The Message of David Swing
to His Generation

The Message of David Swing to His Generation

Addresses and Papers

With an
Introductory Memorial Address by
NEWELL DWIGHT HILLIS

NEW YORK   CHICAGO   TORONTO
Fleming H. Revell Company
LONDON   AND   EDINBURGH

New York: 158 Fifth Avenue
Chicago: 125 North Wabash Ave.
Toronto: 25 Richmond Street, W.
London: 21 Paternoster Square
Edinburgh: 100 Princes Street

Contents

The Message of David Swing

A Memorial Address
By Newell Dwight Hillis

A MEMORIAL ADDRESS[1]
By Newell Dwight Hillis

ASSEMBLED again within these familiar walls, affection claims her rights and memory tells us that now years have passed away since he who was at once our pastor, teacher, sage, and seer gave forth his final word before passing on forever.

For twenty years and more the eager multitudes who loved him thronged and crowded here, where he informed of beauty, traced the rugged truth, gave men vision and divine uplift. And other multitudes there were, whose feet indeed have never trod these aisles, but who were wont to wait each week for his printed words, and when his message closed, they were as desert pilgrims who found the heavenly manna had ceased to fall, the great rock had ceased to flow in cooling streams. Unceasingly with pen and voice did he ply men with motives of culture and duty, seek-

[1] Delivered October, 1895, in Central Church, Chicago, where Professor Swing was succeeded in pastorate by the speaker.

ing by light and darkness, by hope and love to make men patriots, Christians—the veritable sons of God. Oft did he rejoice in our good fortune; full oft was he touched with our griefs; a thousand times he pointed out for us the paths wherein lay the most of happiness and the most of peace; and when at last his great friendly presence was withdrawn from our homes and streets we found ourselves looking with altered eyes upon an altered world.

When the news of his death came, it was with us as with Phillips Brooks when he learned of the death of his friend Richardson, the architect of Trinity Church. In that hour the great preacher turned to the window, and in silence gazed long into the open sky. "It is as if one should wake to find the mountain which one's window had always faced, and upon which one's eyes had always looked, suddenly and forever gone." And now though the first full year is past, the vanished feet still walk with us, the silenced voice still whispers in our dreams. Knitting our brows to the daily task, we have proved that death does exalt those who remain to weep; that our sorrows must ennoble duties, not end them; that our tombs and our tasks are entangled; that the rich blossoms of the heart grow crimson, nourished by our graves. And so we are here to-day to keep a tryst with memory, to remind ourselves of what our friend was; what were the forces and causes that made him so; and by every motive of honour, to pledge ourselves anew to duty, to culture, to beauty, to God, to His divine and human Son who taught His servant how to "dip His sword," not in blood, but "in heaven."

To-day in this presence we remember that the true measure of a city's civilization is the kind of man it reveres and loves. Dying, Lord Bacon said: "I leave my name and fame to foreign lands, and to my countrymen when some time be past." It was to the shame of Florence that a century rolled by before her citizens were able to appreciate the exiled Dante, whose genius redeemed Florence out of meanness and obscurity. Ours is a world where the fathers kill the prophet to whose tomb the children throng in innumerable multitudes. But it is to the lasting praise of our city, and proves how high our society has risen in the scale of refinement and character, that in his lifetime an eager hearing was given to this sage, who spake of pure morals, whose theme was the folly of ignorance and vice, and the supremacy of truth and duty.

We know that eloquence is partly in the orator's charm ; another part is the kindling response of the appreciative hearer. And that generation must have loved the higher life and been touched to the finer issues, that loved this man who was the most refined of American preachers, and whose sermons and essays have a certain grace and delicacy and sweet completeness that make them altogether unique. Always our loves tell us what we are, and foretell what our children are to be. Whenever Providence would order a forward movement of society, He raises up some giant who capitalizes the new spirit. Howard, Garrison, Lincoln compacted in themselves the diffused ideas of philanthropy, reform, liberty, and then flamed these ideas forth upon the common people. Looking to these heroic leaders, soon the multitude went up and took a place beside them.

It seems, therefore, like a special token of divine favour that God sent us this man to capitalize before our people ideas of taste and beauty ; of patriotism, liberty and religion. For not our harbours crowded with ships, not our lakes fringed with forests, not our mines, our factories and our stores stuffed with treasure have been God's best gift to this people: God's best gift has been the gift of great men like Lincoln in statecraft; like Grant in defense of country; like Beecher and Brooks and Swing as teachers of religion. And to-day it is a source of joy and gratitude unspeakable, that here to this new, rude, bustling city Providence sent one who seems like some Plato lifted out of his Athenian groves, and set down in the midst of our booths and markets, to build for us a temple with pure Ionic lines: to light upon its altars the sacred Hebrew flame.

Recognizing his masterful genius, our editors, authors, and people have come to rank David Swing with the great pulpiteers of our generation. Comparing mind with mind, we speak of Spurgeon as devotional, Beecher as philosophical, Brooks as inspirational, Swing as poetical. Seeking a symbol of the qualities of each, we say that Spurgeon was a speaking trumpet, Brooks was a flaming heart, Beecher was a quaking thunderbolt, Swing a singing harp. But when many attempts have been made to

search out the power of this poet-preacher,
his secret still remains a mystery. Until we
know why the rose is sweet, or the sunbeam
light, or the babe divine, we cannot know
why the seer is the best benefactor of humanity.

George William Curtis tells us that while
the poet's power is less dramatic, less obvi-
ous, imposing, and immediate than the power
of the statesman, the warrior, and the inventor, yet his influence is as deep, strong
and abiding. For while the soldier fights
for his native land, the poet clothes that land
with charm and fires the warrior's heart with
energy invincible; while the statesman or-
ganizes liberty, the poet feeds the sacred
fires; while the inventor multiplies the con-
veniences of life, the poet deepens the life-
spring itself. To-day we may not fully un-
derstand the power of our poet and seer, but
we joyfully confess that he revealed to us
our deeper convictions, filled us with fervour
and aspiration, and, in an age of fret and
fume, lifted us into the realm of tranquillity,
through parable and poem teaching us where
were the paths leading unto happiness and
peace.

When Macaulay was shown the vast clustering vine in Hampton Court, with a trunk like unto a tree, he expressed a wish to behold the mother root in Spain from which this scion was cut. Similarly, we confess to an eager desire to trace the ancestral forces that united in this elect child of genius. No great man appears suddenly. Ancestral momentum explains unusual strength. The foot-hills slope upward towards the mountain-minded man. Each Emerson has back of him seven generations of scholars who seem the favourites of heaven. Back of Henry Ward Beecher was a father who was at once a moral hero and an intellectual giant, and a mother who shot the sturdy Beecher type through and through with rich, warm, glowing tones. Thus the students have traced our friend Swing's parentage back to the border-lines of Alsace and Lorraine. There we front the old German stock,—philosophical, scholarly, ponderous, yet mystical and a dreamer of dreams. And over against the German stands the Norman, with a certain lightness and nimbleness of mind—graceful, imaginative, full of rollicking humour—his speech all rippling with sunshine and his lips bubbling over with lyric song. And Providence ordained that all the best qualities of these two types should converge and meet in this poet-preacher. As for the rest, all is veiled. His genius is an unread riddle.

When the explorer has traced the river Nile back to the initial lake he has still fallen short of the source of that mighty stream. Above him in the distant clouds are the secret invisible agencies out of which issue the summer's storms and the winter's snows that fill the springs and crowd the water on in massy flow. And the secret of greatness is partly ancestral, but chiefly divine. God breathes it. Its sources are in that holy of holies where dwell clouds and thick darkness. There God girded this man for his task, and sent him forth with faculties like the prophet's sword.

Searching out the essential qualities of his sermons, an English author has said: "Other sermons are logical or instructive or inspiring, but Swing's always add that element of beauty that turns language into literature." Misunderstanding this æsthetic element, some men have been captious and critical. But with David Swing beauty was no mere mush of æsthetics; no mere love of decoration and ornament. Beauty with him was

16

not the frosting upon the cake; nor veneer upon the world; nor Horace's purple patch upon a humble garment. Beauty was ripeness, soundness, maturity. Ugliness spake of broken laws. He saw that the pink flush upon the cheek of the babe or maiden meant perfect health, and that the muddiness in the drunkard's eye was the sediment of sin. The soft flush upon the plum or purple cluster and the robe of loveliness cast o'er the yellow harvest fields was God's way of saying that His work was done, that things had come to ripeness and touched the limit of their growth.

He knew that when conversation was carried up unto beauty it became eloquence; that knowledge carried up unto beauty became wisdom and refinement; that hut-building carried up unto beauty became temple-rearing; while the man who was just and gentle stood forth before his admiring vision with a moral beauty beyond that of an Apollo. Therefore he revolted from sin as from a form of ugliness and vulgarity. As Shakespeare passed by the vixen and scold to select an *Imogen* or *Rosalind*, as Titian preferred the noble soldier's face before Iago's, dimmed with passion and seamed with sensuality, so with winning grace Swing placed his gentle emphasis upon whatsoever things were lovely, whatsoever things were pure, seeking to bring men unto that harmony and symmetry that betray the beauty of God upon them.

Here in this vast centre of greed and gain, where Mammon threatens to master men, where youth is charmed with the glitter of coin as birds with the glitter of snakes' eyes, where stores and the treasure in them, factories and the wealth by them eclipse the hidden things of the soul, here he stood for twenty years urging that the beautiful is the useful, that life is more than meat, that earth is not a stable, its food not fodder, nor its children beasts, but that man is what he is at his best estate when he dwells in the realm of knowledge and hope and love. Only the next generation can tell how much he did to strengthen those sentiments that manifest themselves in libraries, museums, art-galleries, institutions of higher education. But it is for this generation to be grateful that God saw our city's need, and raised him up to be with others what Bacon calls an "architect of states."

We who love him know that another

striking characteristic was the seer-like quality of his thinking. Many of his sermons were visions into which were gathered all our hopes and aspirations, all our ideals, with their sweet torment and discontent, with their certain triumph and victory. In these higher moods he saw things unseen, dreamed dreams, fought battles, and sometimes perceived afar off that glad day when the columns of society should encamp upon the heights and hang out signals of victory. Nothing proves the creative mind like this imaginative element. Beholding a tree, the strict pragmatist sees nothing but fire-wood. His unit of measurement is a tape-line, and he estimates its moral value in terms of heat and flame. He fears exceedingly when the seer declares that a tree's chief use is to tell of the goings of God among the branches ; that a tree sings hymns and is a hostelry of delight ; that a tree is a living creature,—its song perfume, its words fruit. But the tree presents these aspects, and the seer must tell what he sees.

The imagination is a prophet. It is God's forerunner. It plants hard problems as seeds, rears these germs into trees, and from them gathers the ripe fruit. It wins victories before battles are fought. It works in many realms. Without it civilization would be impossible. Working in things useful it enables Watt to organize his engine; working amid the beautiful, it fashions pictures and rears cathedrals; working with ideas, it creates intellectual systems; working in morals, it constructs ethical systems; working towards immortality, it bids cooling streams, fruitful trees, sweet sounds, all noble friends' lips, report themselves beyond the grave. For faith itself is but the imagination allied with confidence that God is able to realize all our highest ideals.

Without this seer-like element life would be utterly unendurable, and society would perish under sheer weight of drudgery. Each youthful Clay endures the privations of the corn field, each Garfield the pain and poverty of the canal path, because imagination unveils the future and reveals a day when the youth shall build thrones, lead armies, organize laws. And each reformer endures as did the prisoner in the Castle of Chillon. When the little seed sprang up in his cell he saw the tiny plant swell into the stature of a tree; tropical birds sang in its branches; flowers grew over its roots; children were grateful for its shade; storms moved towards it from the distant snow-capped mountains. Imagination enlarged that little plant until it became a forest, and widened the prisoner's cell into a universe. Without imagination no man can become a preacher, and this divine gift was David Swing's. By it he stripped off the hull of dogma and found the sweet kernel. With it he explained riddles. It helped him exalt life's commonplaces. Under its touch moral principles that were dead and uninviting became as dry roots, smitten in summer into fruit and beauty. This preëminent faculty in him turned his sermons into moral poems, pictures, gardens, landscapes. Therefore, also Dr. Barrows' words : " If that which is keyed to universal truth is not to be out-grown, why should not men and women read for generations the thoughts of David Swing ? "

And you who heard him here know that he was a sublime optimist. He believed in the triumph of goodness. Pessimism seemed to him a vulgar form of atheism. He saw God abroad everywhere leavening society as yeast. Growth was the spirit of the ages and the genius of the universe. Looking

backward he saw all creation set forth upon
an upward march. The stars revolved. The
dead crust of the earth rose up into conscious
life. The vegetable kingdom stood erect and
drew near to the animal realm. "The very
beasts felt something stirring in them, and
journeyed upward. Man, too, as if he heard
the music drowsily and afar off, joined the
strange procession and moved upward also."
Afar off he perceived the extinction of ignorance and sin, and the triumph of goodness. That he was not impatient of the slow-
ness of social progress argues his greatness.
Mr. Gladstone once said that the contentment
of the people was largely their blindness to a
better way; that to-day's institutions are
concessions made to ignorance and fear.
When, therefore, we consider that the veil
was lifted before this man's vision so that
he saw a thousand wrongs that might be
righted, a thousand abuses that might be
wiped away, a thousand reforms that should
to-day be achieved, we marvel at his patience,
his buoyancy, his hopefulness, his optimism.
But he stayed himself on God, with whom
"a thousand years are but as one day."

When he saw the church journeying forward in an ox-cart, he foretold the day when

man's heart and conscience should move forward with the speed and comfort with which his body travels. When he saw man dispirited with his own littleness, he whispered that eloquence and art came through great thoughts and themes; that Christianity's vision made Dante; that paradise made Milton; that a madonna made Raphael. And so he fed the hope that the greatness of Jesus Christ would repeat itself in each loving heart, even as the sun sets and repeats its colours in the topaz and ruby. When he saw men discouraged whose secret cry was "No man careth for my soul," who seemed like King Lear driven on in the night, with head white and uncovered before the storm, he pointed these discouraged ones to the golden clouds and the mountain peaks, and urged that above and beyond them was One whose footprints are on the hills, whose song is in the summer, whose bosom is love, whose face and presence will explain all our hard problems.

And when at last he saw men standing about the open grave of falling statesman, dying woman, sleeping child, he whispered that for Lincoln and Tennyson to continue beyond the grave is less wonderful than that

they should enter the cradle; that the hero
and the martyr and the beauteous mother
are not journeying forward under the embrace of divine laws towards a black hole in
the ground, but towards a door that opens
into heaven; that a second life and a read-
justment beyond is the only explanation of
the death angel moving through our streets;
that the Divine Form standing in the shadow
behind man, the divine laws girding man
about, the divine river that sweeps man's
spirit on, the divine affection for dear ones
that strengthens as the body weakens, all
these unite to feed the hope that beyond the
grave there stand Divine Arms outstretched,
waiting to receive man's soul.

The world spake of William Pitt as "the
Great Commoner," because he dealt in the
universal truths of liberty, even as science
deals with universal propositions about land
and sea and sky. Thus, in the realm of
morals, David Swing laid all his emphasis
upon the common-sense principles that are
related to men, not as Protestants or Catholics, but to men as the children of God. He
caused Christianity to stand forth as a simple
single shaft. He saw that when a cathedral
was mingled with booths and shops and

ruined cottages, the grandeur of the temple was injured by surroundings that have in them no greatness. He saw that a mountain surrounded by foot-hills for hundreds of miles was obscured by its very complexity. Recalling St. Peter's, he remembered that the architects were enemies, and that the artists quarrelled bitterly. But the temple grew in grandeur because the columns and arches cast off the quarrels of human life. Rising into the sky it absorbed the genius and love of each architect, but left his strife and his chips to perish below.

He also knew that the human mind working in the realm of theology had been similarly untrustworthy, oft maligning God, full oft bringing Christianity into contempt. Therefore he sought a simple religion. He confined himself to a common-sense statement of universal principles. He saw that God made iron, but not tools; pigments, but not paintings; forests, but not furniture; reason and conscience, but not creeds and politics. But he saw also that thought determined deeds, and that right living comes out of sound thinking. And so instead of beginning at the realm where we know least, and working towards the known, he began with the realm where we know most, and worked towards the unknown. Therefore, spake he of man and his divine possibilities, his social duties, his civil obligations, the development of his reason, the training of his taste and imagination, the enrichment of affection, the culture of heart and conscience. Oft he gave the rambling vine a new support and pruned away the dead and leafless stalk. Many, misunderstanding this, shed bitter tears and filled the air with noise and strife. But he kept at his work, for he loved that vine as much as they, and pruned it that the multitudes might find beneath it their shade and shelter. He remembered that all the great ones of history stood forth in an "alluring atmosphere of genius, truth, and beauty." He knew that man could never worship a defective God. Therefore he sought to cause God, as interpreted by Jesus Christ, to rise before men in such a holy and alluring form that each heart would ask the world to join in its anthem. During his life he sometimes destroyed. But it was only destroying the flower that the fruit might swell, the bursting of the bark that the tree might grow. All his destroying was for the sake of saving.

26

Our city's debt to him cannot be measured. Searching out the beginnings of our institutions, Bancroft says, "We can never disassociate our national greatness and our religious teachers." Guizot said Luther made Germany. Choate believed that Calvin shaped the Swiss Republic. Macaulay found the springs of English literature in the King James version of the Bible. When Spurgeon died Mr. Gladstone was quoted as saying: "This dissenter did more for England than any statesman of his generation." The explanation is, all wealth and material greatness begin in the mental and moral life of the people. Things are first thoughts. The doing that makes commerce begins with the thinking that makes scholars. Tools, railways, cities, books, institutions are but the inner life, crystallizing into material form. Wake up man's taste, and he paints pictures; wake up his reason, and he writes books; wake up his justice, and he works reforms; wake up his conscience, and he cleanses his city from abuses. The beginnings of national greatness are not in things without, but in citizens made fertile and rich in resource.

Happy this city, that produced this man

and enjoyed his presence through this, the most plastic and strenuous period of its history! And happy seer; to whom God has given so great opportunity! Ah, David Swing, David Swing! The memory of thy sweet reasonableness is upon us. Still is thy friendly presence here, like a gentle atmosphere. Oft didst thou charm the fever from our brain, the fear and anxiety from our heart. Full oft thou didst release us from thrall and doubt, seeking ever to make us citizens of God's universe. Thy tireless industry doth rebuke us, until, with the Athenian, we murmur: "The trophies of Miltiades will not let us sleep." Thy courage and thy hopefulness do still inspire us, for as the Scottish warriors in Spain flung the heart of the Bruce far into the hosts of the Saracens, and by bravery reclaimed it, so thou didst fling thy heart forward to "the feet of the Eternal," and in death found it again. Here and now we recall thy early struggles; the harsh winds that did assail thy bark; thy nights of study; the eager youth crowding about you in that far-off college; the multitudes that for years flowed in hither with goings like the sound of many waters; the ideals thou didst have for this great city, for its libraries, its galleries, its museums, its homes, its people. To-day a sense of debt is upon us. For the great love we bear thee, we pledge ourselves anew to truth, toleration, and charity, to liberty and fidelity, to conviction, to the poor, to the slave and the savage, to Jesus Christ thy Saviour, to God thy Father. May learning like thine abide ever in our libraries. May goodness like thine ever lend glory to all our chapels. May thy all-perceiving reason, thy all-judging reason, hallow our council chambers. May eloquence lend glory to our forum and pulpit. May heaven drop thy charmed gifts upon our children and our children's children, until all are Christians and patriots. And we will give thee gratitude, and greet thee beyond.

The Message of David Swing

Addresses and Papers
American

I

WASHINGTON AND LINCOLN, I

IN this month of February come the birthdays of our Nation's two greatest men.
The twelfth and twenty-second days of this
month will forever take this time of wintry
deadness and hand it over to all the tropical
luxuriance of a grateful and loving memory,
and make it lie in the confines of perpetual
spring. Flowers that winter denies these
days, the Nation will supply from its heart.

Great sky-watchers those two! Such as
Christ outlined. They illustrate the text [1]
and the whole character of the Man of
Nazareth. As Jesus said : Do not suffer
your thoughts and feelings to pause in the
evening and morning colours of the horizon
made by your little hills and fields and skies,
but upon those spectacles of nature permit
your souls to step upward until you shall
mark what kind of a day ought to come or

[1] Matthew xvi. 3 : Ye can discern the face of the sky,
but can ye not discern the signs of the times ?

is coming to the land which the Hebrews consecrated in their prayers and holy psalms, and which the Roman legions have brought to such desolation—so these two modern minds obey the Master, and rise up as illumined pictures of the old lesson. And the one standing in the valley of the Potomac, the other standing in the sea-like prairies far away, rested not in the scenes of nature as painted on forest and hill, grass and sky, but passing from these to the mightier scenery of man, his state, his church, his home, his library, they gave their minds and powers to a mighty work, and as though reading all the redness and wonder and beauty of the sky, they said in perfect unison: To-day it will be stormy; to-morrow it will be fair!

According to all the biographers of Jesus, He was a great admirer of the means granted to man for forming some acquaintance with his world. He thought the eye and ear worth cultivating and using. If any man had eyes for a special purpose he ought to bring them into daily use. If any man had ears he ought to be continually listening, for the very fact of the eye and ear was a proof ample that there would always be around man something to be seen and heard.

34

The Darwinians hold the theory that the first forms of animal life did not possess such senses as the eye and the ear; that the external world contained so much light and so many things to be seen and contained so many things to be heard that these outside objects in their effort to get into the human brain wore away at last the coverings of the hidden intellect, and made such openings as those which admit scenes and sounds. Inasmuch as matter preceded the mind, it was necessary for the evolutionists to find some method by which light could make an eye and sound make an ear. Thus a demand for an eye created the supply of nerves and lenses and eyelids.

The religious mind assumes two notions: that a God made a wonderful world, and then that He gave man those senses which may enable him to sustain many relations to the great surrounding wonder. Happy man, that his eye can all lifelong sweep over such a horizon of land, water and sky, and that his ear can note myriads of tones from the deep sound of thunder to the song of a bird and the words of an orator or a friend! So amazing are these two powers that persons have wondered whether, if they must part with one of them, they would rather be deaf or blind. In such an hour of indecision each sense seems of infinite worth. From these two forms of mental power came the old wonderment that there should be any person who having eyes should refuse to see their world, and having ears should refuse to hear it. What is true of the eye is true of the whole mind and true of the heart. It must be thought singular that a creature should possess a mind without using it. Its use ought to be as natural as the drinking of water when man is thirsty, or the eating of food when he is hungry.

It ought alone to follow that the rational being having eyes will try to see the most impressive spectacle, and having ears will attempt to hear the most interesting or thrilling sounds. Why gaze at a clod when by raising the eye you can see a rainbow or an ocean ? Why listen to a rattling, empty wagon when by passing into a capitol one might hear a Clay or a Webster ? Standing amid the endless prodigality of scenes and sounds man must be an eclectic. He must separate the great from the small, the melody from the discord.

Christ illustrated His own proposition. He

came into Judæa and at once saw it and
heard it. He came into the great Roman
Empire—that aggregate of a hundred millions
of souls, that vast bulk of Eastern and Western literature, politics, and religion—and in
a few years He saw all and heard all. He
saw the arrogance of things; the degrada-
tion of the people, the tears of women and
children, the errors about God; He heard all
the uproar of the race, the din made out of
the laughter of the wicked, and the groans
of the oppressed. He seemed to say : Why
should I stand here and not see the mighty
vision and not hear the mingled discord and
music ?

The month of February always recalls
two men who having eyes saw and having
ears heard. They selected the greatest scenes
and the sweetest music. They were to make
a short visit and be gone. They wisely
looked around them and listened for what
was greatest in their day. They selected
enough goodness and greatness to make
their birthdays sacred to a great nation.

When these two men were children they
began to see and hear the truths and needs
of their nation. It is not explanation enough
to say that great ideas were already " in the

air." We know that all great minds which had ever lived had spoken some word in behalf of equal rights and personal liberty. From Plato to Dante the eulogy of freedom had been perennial. That stream of truth had indeed been reduced by many a desert, but it had never gone dry. It was seen by Shakespeare and John Milton. It had become large in the times of Pitt and Burke. But few were the minds which could see clearly this noble truth of our race. The lightning had played upon the clouds for thousands of years before a Franklin came to look up with eye wide open. Antigone had seen her blind father sink down under a crash of thunder; Virgil had seen the sky all ablaze with this rapid fire. Thus for ages had the thunder-storms flashed and roared over the nations. At last came one with a series of questions to be asked of the clouds and their dazzling light. It is not enough that freedom was in the air. We must love the men who caught the fugitive and gave it to a continent.

When we think about such men as these two February names, we must dismiss the words " fate " and " destiny " and give them the credit of that choice which made them so great. They deliberately chose to see and hear their country. It is a sad universe if hell or heaven is assigned to man by blind fate. If the Emperor Nero was on a moral level with St. John and St. Paul, then is our world a failure. Man is then without praise or blame. But if the mind can select a noble form of being and conduct, then the world becomes the arena of patriots and saints and is the vestibule of a possible paradise.

In such a universe of a God and a divine choice society must run to the Washingtons and Lincolns, and throw at their feet the wreaths befitting their lives. This splendour is all their own. We cannot repair to the banks of the Potomac or to the wilds of Kentucky to take anything away. We must go thither only to thank the two mortals for seeing and hearing the passing centuries. These two men were at liberty to live worthless or injurious lives. Washington was at liberty to become a Benedict Arnold; Mr. Lincoln was at liberty to become a slave-driver or a common idler. We must honour the two men for becoming the friends of their race.

These two men, taken together, compose a most complete lesson of life. The latter

lesson came to supplement the defects of the
former. Washington was the child of good
fortune, Lincoln the child of adversity ; and
yet they came to one greatness, as if to teach
our generation that no wealth or poverty
need separate the heart from great principles.
Washington had everything, Lincoln nothing. From these facts it is to be inferred
that the good mind may move in its own
name. If it cannot ride in a chariot it can
go on foot.

As wealth was measured a hundred years
ago the young Washington was rich in
money. He was surrounded by scholars.
All those first families of Virginia loved a
kind of moral and literary greatness. This
high style was perhaps imported by Sir
Walter Raleigh himself who was a highly
educated adventurer, anxious to be in perfect
accord with the age of Queen Elizabeth.
After Raleigh, a large number of families
brought to Virginia what might be called
the intellectual style. In our day the old
mental scene seems full of stiffness and
pomposity, but by the time young Washington came upon the stage the old vanity
had reached nearer to the level of natural-
ness ; yet could the picture be compared with

the portrait of our day it would seem a group of wooden men and women moved by machinery. All talked in a calm, rhetorical style. All table talk was carried on in the language of oratory. Love letters were composed in the measured sentences of the philosophers. The oldest brother of Washington was sent to Oxford to be educated because there was in the Colonies no school that was worthy of the presence and tuition fees of such a noble Virginian. After the return of this Lawrence, George, a mere lad, lived in the presence of an Oxford graduate, and must have absorbed a large quantity of the wisdom and culture of the best town of old England. Thus surrounded by mental and moral influence, George became quite a student of conduct, and when he was entering upon the world of fashion and society at large he wrote out a set of rules which should regulate him in his trip through the multitude of men and women. His father, his mother, his brother, his uncles, his neighbours were all of one type and that type marked by morality, politeness and a certain colossal pride.

Contrast with such a boyhood the early years of Abraham Lincoln. It would pain our hearts should we attempt to recall all the particulars of that life in Kentucky, Indiana and Illinois. As if one would not suffice, that youth tasted the rudeness of three wild States. When the poverty of Kentucky became intolerable the family made a long, exhaustive journey to the poverty of Indiana; and when the soul wearied of that bitterness the family loaded all things into an ox-wagon and moved through long and deep mud to find the extremest hardship of early Illinois. The moving Lincoln family recalls the verses of Isaac Watts about the sick man who in pain often turned over in his sick bed, but at each turn took his disease over with him.

Recall the young Washington with his bright knee-buckles; with his great Oxford brother by his side; the air around them full of splendour, of culture and ambition: recall the young Lincoln following with bare feet a migrating ox-cart, which was simply rolling along from the deep mud of Indiana to the same kind of mud further West.

The picture of Lincoln would be more tolerable if the poverty had attended the youth only in his minority, but it refused to leave the kind-hearted man and assailed him without mercy for almost a half century. His day was darkened not only by poverty but by other clouds.

Of that stay of fifty-seven years upon earth only the last ten were touched with any of the earth's kindness and beauty. It is no wonder Mr. Lincoln carried a sad face, for it is known that the face is shaped by the heart. As thorns and thistles do not produce great bunches of grapes, so long years of cloud cannot throw much sunshine on the cheek and forehead. The cruel murder of April 14, 1865, completed the long chain of grief. The clouds opened once and let fall a little sunshine upon the man's soul, but after those few beams came a swift darkness. In sorrow the last hour was in harmony with the first. The tune of his spirit ended on the sad note with which it began. Of all great names in the modern roll-call that of Abraham Lincoln is fullest of pathos. Great but sorrowful, smiling through tears, he was murdered in his only day of a personal blessedness.

Our Nation ought to be glad that it contains these two forms of biography. Passing down the times together they sweep the whole field of American life and assure all our youth that neither riches nor poverty must interfere with the race of the soul towards success. If our land possessed only the memory of the man from Illinois it might feel that no great man can ever come except by the way of bare feet and a mauling of rails. With the daily spread and advance of riches, hope of future great men might decline and fade. Our youth would seem too happy in poverty ever to become great in mind. What a poor world this would be if only those who are barefooted and bareheaded might run along the paths of knowledge and fame! And what a poor world it would be if those who are barefooted were forbidden to walk or run in those flowery roads! But what a good world it is, if it looks at only the faces of those who run and never cares whether the feet are unclad or are bright with slippers of pure gold!

The crowns of the mental empire are not in waiting for either riches or poverty. Plato was rich, Socrates poor, but philosophy could not see these distinctions; she ran joyfully to both. Parrhasius dressed in purple and gold, Epictetus in the raiment of a slave; but art and wisdom none the less ran to both these gifted people of the far past. To our age came Washington and Lincoln to teach our youth that greatness and usefulness care nothing for wealth or poverty. They study only the face, the heart. If the eye sees, nature fills it with great scenes; if the ear hears, nature fills it with melody.

Aurelius was a Roman Emperor, Æsop a beggar, but the sky did not care; it conferred upon both the same immortality. The one essential thing is that the heart in youth shall cry out, "I see the world; I hear it!" These two American children met this demand, and from standpoints more than fifty years apart they read deeply the lesson spread before them by their country. The one looked and saw a foreign throne seeking to rule and subjugate the New World and prevent the spread of freedom; the other looked and saw slavery working its way westward, and threatening to make negro bondage the watchword of the Nation. These young eyes opened wide, never again to be closed until by the hand of death. Although the death-beds were separated by two generations, each patriot died amid the shouts of a new, triumphant liberty. The Nation on its memorial days looks back and

sees two young men rising up out of their
tumultuous times. It forgets the abundant
stores of the one, the wretched poverty of
the other, and sees only the two faces, radiant with one intelligence and one love.
Times and customs have undergone great
changes since these two great Americans
died. Wealth has come and political tumult
has passed away. The peace and unity
which the heroes made brought wealth to
the people and took away that old struggle
over liberty which had once made such a
company of great men. Industry, inventions,
great discoveries, land abundant and rich,
combined to exalt all the little pleasures which
money can purchase, and to conceal many a
great form of mental service and destiny.

The value of peace depends upon what
comes after it. When peace is followed by
the pursuit of money and pleasure then the
biographer must find his great subjects in the
days of war; but when war is followed by
public education and public wisdom, then
the historian calls those years a golden age,
and war is left far behind as the thunder-
storm at night is left behind by the spark-
ling morning which follows it in high June!
Our day is depending wholly upon that young

generation which is now following the dead
and which has the opportunity in full to
transform iron into gold. What avail the
ox-teams which can break up the wild prairie
unless men are to follow and sow good wheat
and women are to follow and plant flowers?
After the grave of the Washingtons new
principles must be found. New eyes must
see new happiness. The eye must again see
its world. Its vision must not be clouded by
either poverty or riches. If the young mind
cannot see great visions the world will at
last say to it: Alas that youth was born
blind!

It is often lamented by the churchmen
that Washington and Lincoln possessed little
religion except that found in the word
"God." All that can here be affirmed is
that what the religion of those two men
lacked in theological details it made up in
greatness. Their minds were born with a
love of great principles. Washington loved
and exalted each great principle. He was
compelled by his nature to select from Christianity its central ideas. This tendency was
intensified by the local friendship for France.
France was battling against a vast bundle of
false, Christian particulars. The Colonies so

hated England and so admired France that most of our early statesmen reduced Christianity to that French rationalism which was quite well satisfied with the doctrine of a Creator. A superstitious Christianity was falling to pieces, and the new orthodoxy had not yet come. Many of these statesmen, when they took any steps at all in the path of religion, walked with God alone.

Mr. Lincoln also came seeking principles. His mind could see greatness at a glance. In the wilds of Kentucky and Indiana he had seen at revivals young men and young women preparing to shout. He had seen the deacons and elders removing the coat and extra clothing from the young man, and the mothers arranging some young girls that these converts might for an hour or two move the upper and lower worlds with their motions and shoutings. The present rationalized, orthodox church had not come. It was not in sight. The Presbyterians saw many of their converts fall in a trance ; the Methodists shouted, and depended upon what they called "the power." There were no kind words for those rational minds which asked for a simple religion of worship and righteousness. The Church mistook reason for infidelity and hostility. Mighty changes have come since those two graves were made.

There are few instances in which a mind great enough to reach great principles in politics has been satisfied with a fanatical religion. The Cavour who emancipated Italy became broad in religion when he became great in politics. The Castelar who fed out great truths to Spain reached the same greatness of faith. It must not be asked for Washington and Lincoln that having reached greatness in political principles they should have loved littleness in piety. It is probable that living in our day these two men would have found peace in that new Christianity which is passing along in so much of truth and beauty. Neither of these eminent men possessed enough of poetry to have made him worship like a Newman or a St. John; but in our day their estimate of God would have passed as being an adequate faith for a statesman. Lincoln possessed something of the poetic sentiment, but what of this delicacy lay in either soul was trampled to death under the horses and chariots of war. When Mars reaches out his bloody hand the Muses sit down and weep. The daughters of Zion hang up their harps, and refuse to sing in a bloody land.

February 12th will recall the most illustrious name in history, but it will awaken thought in vain unless it shall induce the youth to march through the past into the present and through the present up to the future. Memory is most useful when it empties its riches into the urns of hope. The past must be the musician for the morrow. Washington saw great principles and out of them he created the happiness of millions. The war did not create him, for he was selecting principles before war came. Before the seven years of battle he had been extracting power from forty years of common life. The clouds of war did not make his soul's rainbow, they only revealed it. Our eyes are so poor and weak that we cannot see the seven colours of the mind unless there is a black cloud behind them. Washington made his character out of the world's common sunshine; he used it in the storm.

Around the feet of this new generation lies to-day a world of mental and moral principles. The Church is coming upon them, the State is finding them like gold-dust hidden in the earth. As men in the classic lands are flinging aside dust and ashes, and are exhuming temples, statues, and jewels, so men of mind are passing below the dust of the centuries and are lifting up into the air and light truths of a divine beauty. So vast are these hidden stores of thought that we must conclude both politics and Christianity to be only in the early morning of their career.

But we have come to a new crisis. It is not to be inquired now what will the deepest poverty do? What salvation will the railsplitter bring? What genius will be born to us out of Kentucky dust? We know the kindness of earth in this one direction. A more pensive inquiry is found in the wonderment what salvation and blessings the rich children are about to bring. Are their estates destined like those of young Washington to turn into moral and intellectual splendour?

In high agriculture the fields must not always grow one kind of grass or grain. The soul dies under such a tax upon one kind of its virtues. Thus society must renew its life and inspiration and when the fathers have amassed gold, the children should not slay

the rich land which produced the harvest
but they should change the growing and
make the next summer time blend with the
fruits and grains of every art, every virtue,
every hope.

Under such magical changes the plains of
humanity cannot become a desert; like the
valley of the Nile, they will become richer
at each overflow of the advancing human
race.

The earth's possibilities are so great that
it will tax the genius of both poverty and
wealth to disclose them. Eminent women
are lamenting that woman's world will seem
so small in any world-wide display of works
and talents. But how could it be infinite?
She was a powerless slave until yesterday.
Over the gateway of her temple she ought
to write the words: "The Works of One
Day of Liberty." But man has a long, long
history, over most of which he ought to sit
down and weep. He has for the most part
chosen to see what was least glorious. It is
to be hoped that he is penitential at least;
and that millions of youths are in mind
and soul following those faces which, human
in America and other lands and divine in
Judæa, are looking up, and with the eye see-

ing all the great spectacles of God and man, and with the ear hearing all the hymns of religion and all the great melodies and symphonies of human life.

II

WASHINGTON AND LINCOLN, II

WHILE our Nation grows older and adds to its moral worth as rapidly as to its passing years, its memorial days will become more significant, and no statesman or editor or clergyman will pass unconsciously such graves as those of Washington and Lincoln. The Greeks and Latins celebrated the death-days of their great men because greatness did not reach its climax at the cradle, but nearer the tomb. Our country, in regarding the birthdays of its distinguished sons, has in heart the same feelings which the classics cherished, and uses the joy and beauty of the cradle only as an emblem of the subsequent splendour of life. Any day taken from that career which ended in 1799—such as the day in October when Cornwallis surrendered to Washington—would answer as well as the day in February for a trumpet-call to awaken an unequalled memory. Be the hour that of cradle or inauguration or farewell address or grave, it recalls the one great historic fact—the man.

The American habit of taking up the birthday as an emblem of the whole page or volume in history is well, for there the first smile of life is seen and the cradle is less sad than the sepulchre. This smallest month in the year is ornamented by the two greatest birthdays recorded upon our continent—those of Washington and Lincoln. February 12th will by degrees become the associate in love and memory of February 22d, and both will advance in honour with the advance of public patriotism and culture.

Only ten years lay between the death of Washington and the birth of Abraham Lincoln. In that little interregnum the people ruled just as they do now when both kings have long been absent from the land they loved. But we should all see to it that the absence is only that of the material form, not that of the soul. The bookmaker, the journalist, the politician, the preacher, the poet, and the painter should carry onward the spirit of these men and make them to be the same moral forces in the morrow they were in the yesterday. What the old saints are to Christianity these two patriots are to our country. Take from beneath our churches the Christ and the Saints Paul and John, and although each truth of a natural religion would remain, what a coldness would be felt in the walls! How hearts would freeze at the altars! So our Nation does not repose upon only abstract ideas, but also upon the warm hearts which once beat along the Potomac and in the prairies of Illinois.

Society is moved, but also held by its attachments, and doubly fortunate and successful is it when its attachments bind it to the best truths. Men love their country, right or wrong; but fortunate is our Nation in that its great heroic characters were in perfect harmony with the most refined light, and thus truth and sentiment are in full partnership. There have been states which have had to apologize for the defects of their heroes—their Cæsars or Napoleons or Georges—their emperors or queens or czars; but fortunate was this February in those two cradles over which attachment and philosophy join in unusual concord. Love sees nothing that need be forgiven. Patriotism and reason meet over these birthdays and, willing to love country, right and wrong, men may love it all the more in this unsullied memory of right.

Next to the saints of religion must be ranked in all our minds these saints of our country; because our Nation asks not for political theory only, but for a worship, a friendship that can conquer and hope like the faith of the Christians. When an enemy rises up against this Republic it must always find not a mere soulless corporation, but a passion, a sentiment which will pluck up trees by the root and toss mountains into the sea. A mother defends her child not only because of right and principle, but also because of her affection. Thus great, pure leaders, like those of historic memory, enlarge political philosophy into devotion. It helped our Nation in its dark days of 1776 and 1861 that its two leaders were so worthy of admiration. The soldiers of Valley Forge saw in their general a lofty character for whom they could endure privations, in whom they could trust. When they were cold and hungry and homesick they were still inspired by the merit of their commander. He had separated himself from his wealth and its peace to be a soldier against the greatest power upon earth; the troops saw of that moral worth and were cheered by the vision when all other scenes were darkened.

When Baron Steuben, an ardent volunteer from the German army, saw the troops at Valley Forge, their wants of all the comforts of life, he wondered what held the soldiers so firmly to their post of duty. It was a moral power that held them—the hope of a free nation and faith in their chieftain. In Philadelphia the British army, from the highest to the humblest, was spending in carousal the winter months which the colonial troops were spending in all forms of discomfort. One British officer kept a gambling house in which the common soldiers were robbed of their gold. Thus was the British army a military machine, while an American army was a band of men, with a soul in it—an army of 6,000 friends of freedom and of Washington. Washington's dining-room of logs, a banqueting hall that could be duplicated for fifty dollars, where there was simple food and no carousal, became an emblem of the kind of leader the rank and file was trusting and following. This scene was repeated in the war of secession. Whatever the hardships of the soldiers in that long and awful war, the troops could always think of Abraham Lincoln as being in full sympathy with them as knowing what labour and privation were, and as being willing to die, if need be, for the welfare of the country. The fame of other men arose and fell, but Mr. Lincoln's shone with a steady beam, however dark the night. All the simplicity and honesty of his character, the hardships of his early life, added to the impressiveness of his name. His history made him the basis of songs and of a deep admiration.

It is wonderful that two such men, so similar, so grand in intellect and morals, came to our Nation in its hour of greatest need. The need did not create them; it simply found them. George Washington was just as honest and noble when he was twenty, and twenty years before the Independence, as he was in the Revolution. When discontent about rank and pay sprang up in the Indian war, Major Washington, then twenty-two, said he would as soon serve as a private as serve as an officer, and for small pay as for large pay; that he would remain with his regiment on the Ohio under any possible arrangement. Thus the subsequent Revolution did not make Washington; it found him.

Thus came Abraham Lincoln into our country, not created by the war of the rebellion, but created previously in the mysterious laboratory of nature. He was simple in life, clear in his views of right and duty, firm in his will, long before the flag of war was unfurled. Circumstances ought to have made a hero and patriot out of James Buchanan, but they were unequal to the large task; they ought to have fashioned a leader out of Stephen A. Douglas, but they could not teach him the whole of the right as to Territories where no slave had ever been. Circumstances did not fit Wendell Phillips nor Mr. Garrison for the highest office, for neither of them could have carried that heart of justice towards the South which the times required. Many men came near being worthy, but some valuable element seemed wanting until this singular character was led up out of the high grass of Illinois. He was a marvellous combination of intellectual power and of the sentiment of right. An English reporter who had come to this country expressly to ridicule Mr. Lincoln for an English paper (the London *Punch*), after the

President's martyrdom confessed his poor estimate of the Western woodsman:

" My shallow judgment I had learned to rue,
    Noting how to occasion's height he rose ;
How this quaint wit made home-truth seem more true,
    How, iron-like, his temper grew by blows ;

" How humble, yet how hopeful, he could be ;
    How, in good fortune and in all, the same;
Not bitter in success, nor boastful he,
    Thirsty for gold, nor feverish for fame.

" He went about his work—such work as few
    Ever had laid on head and heart and hand—
As one who knows, where there's a task to do,
    Man's honest will must heaven's good grace command ;

" The words of mercy were upon his lips,
    Forgiveness in his heart and on his pen,
When this vile murderer brought swift eclipse
    To thoughts of peace on earth, good will to men.

" The Old World and the New, from sea to sea
    Utter one voice of sympathy and shame.
Sore heart, so stopped when it at last beat high !
    Sad life, cut short just as its triumph came ! "

Great memory of our country, that in ten years after the death of Washington, this child was opening its eyes upon a continent that was to make him a part of its second great drama !

The Message of David Swing

So far is our day from the time of Washington, that many details have fallen out of the picture, and there remains the form without the life. To the new generation that man, once called the "Saviour of His Country" and the "Father of His Country," has become as dead and cold as a marble statue of some ancient Greek or Roman. The calm forehead and noble face remain, but that human nature—which still comes to us when the name of Lincoln is pronounced—has fallen away from Washington. But this is not time's fault, it is the fault of the new generation: for God has made the mind such that it can recall past years and fill itself with living pictures. Nature offers no reward to mental indolence. It hates an idler in any field. If the passion for property has injured all love of literature and if so far as literary taste remains it prefers a foolish novel to the greatest pages of history, certainly in such an age a few years will blot out scenes the most wonderful and events the most thrilling. The law of nature is that to the industrious mind pursuing the best paths, the past shall be made almost as vivid as the present. Not eighteen hundred years ago can destroy the picture of the living Jesus; a hundred years cannot turn into dead rock the Fathers of the Nation.

Man is the only animal to which nature has granted the power of seeing the past. The brute lives by the day; but each educated soul carries hundreds of years in the heart. Thus life is endeared, and the youth of twenty may seem to be living in a day thirty centuries in length. But all this landscape depends for its breadth and beauty upon the mind's activity. When one comes to the Mississippi one may see only a muddy stream, or he can behold that stream with De Soto at its mouth and red men on its banks three hundred years ago; and when the same heart comes to the Potomac it may see only the fishing-boys and the negroes idle in the sun, or it may see Washington there in those days whose sun went down a hundred years before the sun of this sacred morning came. Man's present is only an hour or two, but when his mind is awakened the past and future are melted into the present and make each passing hour great in all its associations and hopes.

Not all minds may indeed possess the same power of recalling the past, but the common mental attributes are quite uniformly distrib-

uted, and few are the young persons of to-
day who could not, if so they wished, recall
the bygone times until they could hear the
leaves rustle, in the autumn, under the foot
of George Washington, could hear the axe of
young Lincoln sounding afar in the lonely
woods, could even see Jesus of Nazareth in
His cottage in the Galilean hills or in the
streets of Jerusalem. God made the soul too
great to lie poised upon the present moment.
It should rest upon the past and the future.
But if the mind possesses no activity, or if
its activity is exhausted upon transient and
worthless literature, the past falls out of life
and all the grand ones from the Divine Christ
to the human Washington and Lincoln are
only names without any meaning. Often are
they made the subjects of ridicule or wit by
hearts that have never measured the greatness of the lives for which the names stand.
The philosophy of that revival of interest in
the birthdays of our two greatest men is the
hope that the new generation may grasp the
past of the Nation and may pass from ignorance to knowledge and from silly ridicule to
deep admiration.

One of the best lessons to be read from these
two names is the warmth of their hearts.

There was no indifference in these two characters. Great as their minds were, they were also powerful in their affections. Washington suffers now from the peculiar dignity of the old literary style. That style, perfected by Addison and Johnson, made a letter from friend to friend as pompous as a President's message or a King's address to a Parliament. Hamilton, George Washington, and Martha, each man and woman, used the style of Edmund Burke; and a love-letter read like an oration. But translating Washington's letters into the simple English of to-day, he is seen at once to have been a man of deep love, with his country one of the chief objects of his passion. The kindness and pathos of Mr. Lincoln are better seen because they are expressed in the dialect of our time, while the same qualities in Washington are toned down by the stateliness of the Miltonian English. When Washington had bidden good-bye to Lafayette he followed the noble French patriot with a letter which shows the tenderness of the American's heart:

"In the moment of our separation, upon the road as we travelled and every hour since, I have felt all the love, respect and attach-

ment for you with which length of years,
close connection, and your merits have inspired me. I often asked myself as our carriages separated whether that was the last
sight I should ever have of you. My fears
answered yes. I called to mind the days of
my youth, that they had long fled to return
no more; that I was now descending the hill
I had been fifty-two years in climbing, and
that although I was blessed with a good
constitution I was of a short-lived family and
might soon expect to be entombed in the
mansion of my fathers. These thoughts
darkened the shades and gave a gloom to the
picture and consequently to my prospect of
seeing you again." Strip this letter of its
stateliness and it recalls a tearful carriage
ride from Mt. Vernon to Annapolis. Washington and Lafayette journeying towards the
harbour whence the great friend of freedom
was to sail for France, riding along mile after
mile, in the Indian summer of Maryland,
make a picture which is easily filled with all
the friendship and nobleness and pathos of the
once real life. It does not ask for much
imagination to bring that good-bye ride so
near and real as to make the rattle of the
carriages audible and the slow procession

visible on a long hillside, and thus visible are
the travellers.

It is of fresh memory that Mr. Lincoln
was a man of unusual warmth of heart—a
twofold reminder in these two names that
our age asks for men not of vast wealth and
of endless political acuteness but men who
can love the country and be once more as a
father full of affection for all the household.
Men without affection for their nation make
citizens like Benedict Arnold, Aaron Burr, or
the advocates of Anarchy or political frauds.
The country needs only those children who
are capable of studying the great pages of
history and of forming tender attachments for
all that is good in our national career. It is
the evil of our day that the human heart has
passed out of power, and that machine
natures have attempted to fill up the tremendous vacancy. The Treasury at Washington
is full but the Nation's heart is empty. The
rights of the negro are not secured to him ;
the tremendous frauds of corporations are
permitted to go on with a growing robbery
of the people, and all because the love of the
whole country is inactive and men of great
brain have displaced the men of large soul.
This disease of the political heart is so in-

fectious that we all are touched with its blight, and look upon our country as only a soulless corporation.

But our government is not a corporation. It is a vast family of dependent ones where hearts and hands should be joined for mutual welfare. Washington and Lincoln being absent, the Congress and the President stand *in loco parentis,* and should carry onward all that old sympathy with the people which made all the old glory of our fathers. A colonial officer once wrote to Washington, suggesting that, in case independence was secured, they establish an American king; that the people could never rule. Washington quickly wrote to the young aristocrat never to speak or even think of such a result again—that the coming government must be that of the people. Thus was he the people's friend, and now that these States are occupied by fifty millions of people, the need of a friend has not undergone any decline. These millions are not rich nor powerful, they need a government which can secure to them "life, liberty and the pursuit of happiness."

That our country is not a cold corporation may be read from the peculiar concomitants in its progress. Our national hymns betray a national soul. Had the old East India Company any hymns? Has any corporation in our land any great dead, any heroic graves, where students and benefactors stand to ponder and admire? Have these corporations any eloquence like that of Patrick Henry, Henry Clay, Daniel Webster, and of Lincoln at Gettysburg? Have they any self-denial like that of the soldiers who fell at Yorktown or in the Wilderness? Have they any poetry like "The Star-Spangled Banner"? Have they any torn and powder-stained battle-flags? Hear these words, a part of a vast hymn:

> " Oft o'er the seaman's or the soldier's bier
>   Droops the dear banner for his glittering pall,
>   Where every star might seem an angel's tear,
>   And every stripe Christ's mercy covering all.

> " See from the rampart how the freshening breeze
>   Flings out that flag of splendour, where the Night
>   Mingles with flaming Day its blazonries,
>   And spreads its wavy azure, star-bedight."

Did ever the noblest corporation—the London Bank—did the meanest in the world ever fly such a holy banner, and compose such words of eulogy? Ah, no! Our

country is not a corporation; it is a sentiment also, like that which binds the inmates
of a home all into one love through life and
death.

Washington and Lincoln should stand as
proofs forever that our Nation is a great
beating heart, capable of many sorrows and
a many-coloured happiness; a great heart
like that of Jesus, which must embrace millions in its measureless affections, and love
all equally. All the struggles and disap-
pointments and labours of Washington, all
the similar pains and tears of Lincoln tell
us that when we come to the words "our
country" we have come to a living soul,
that ought to be as omnipotent as the hand
of God, as loving and pure as the heart of
Jesus, the Son of God and of all humanity.

Washington came up from Virginia,
Lincoln down from Illinois; both came in
one spotless honour, in one self-denial, in
one patience and labour, in one love of man:
both came in the name of one simple Christianity; both breathing daily prayers to
God,—thus came, as though to picture a
time when Virginia and Illinois, all the
South and all the North, would be alike,
—one in works, in love, in religion, and in

all the details of national fame. If any of you young hearts have begun to forget your Nation and its heroes, you would better sit down by her rivers and remember your lost Zion, and weep as the old vision unveils itself, and then pray God to let your right hand forget its cunning rather than permit your soul to empty itself of your country.

III

JAMES A. GARFIELD[1]

IN that part of our earth which was made memorable by the presence of Jesus many of the cities and towns were located upon the summit of a hill or mountain. The oppressive temperature of the summer months, and military considerations, and also a sense of the beautiful led those who were about to found a village or a city to seek not always some river-bank or lake-shore, but some hill or crag or mountain. Nazareth, the town of Christ's early life, was on a height, and on one side there was a fearful precipice down which the offended citizens threatened to throw Him who had rebuked their sins. The two mountains, Moriah and Sion, remind us that Jerusalem was seated upon lofty heights and was a grand spectacle to the traveller who was journeying thither in its palmy days. The Temple of Solomon,

[1] President Garfield was shot by a disappointed office-seeker July 1 ; died September 19, 1881.

the palaces of the king and his court, with the walls and watch-towers, made up an impressive scene to all coming along the valleys of Kedron and Hinnom, and fully justified the thought of Christ that "a city set on a hill cannot be hid."

The domain of Christ was spiritual; when He spoke of material things He had the spiritual qualities of our world in His mind. He wished that His disciples might possess virtues so great and so active that all society might behold and enjoy their righteousness and benevolence. The ages had been full of diminutive persons who lived only for self and for all small results—persons like to lighted candles placed under a bushel. It was time other forms of soul should appear, time for the world to have minds and hearts that should be as large and visible as cities upon mountains. Soon after the great Palestine Teacher had uttered His wish, and had given the nations a specimen of a soul too large and too lofty to be concealed, the dream began to find fulfillment in many of the departments of human life. Thought and sentiment began to be enlarged, history began to record greater actions and to receive into its storehouse greater biographies.

There came along in the living tide men whose heads rose above the multitude like the tall cliff which "midway leaves the storm."

Our Nation mourns to-day the loss of one too lofty to be concealed. All the grades of society, looking up from the door of cottage or palace, see this outline of a scholar, a statesman, and soldier and president, and all mourn that the image is no longer to be seen in life, but only in death's pallor. The spectacle is made unusual not only by the merit of the man who has died, but also by the savage cruelty of the wound that robbed this citizen of his existence. The eighty days of physical and mental suffering, of alternate hope and fear, days which reduced a powerful man to the powers of only an infant, add their awful part towards placing his name fully before the civilized portion of the world. Made conspicuous by his character and works, Mr. Garfield becomes conspicuous by his misfortune. Thus this figure stands as upon a hill, and it will require centuries full of men and of events to hide its colossal outline from the gaze of mankind. Man is drawn towards the pathetic. What touches his heart touches also his memory. Pity often makes up a large element in love. Had Mr. Garfield died of disease or by the limitation of nature he would have been a large subject of study, but millions will read his biography in coming years because it ends in the awful cloud of tragedy. What do we witness today, and what will those behold who shall in future times run over the black and white page in history, black with misfortune, white in virtue? It must come to us as a peculiar fact that two of the greatest of American names are now made more sacred by the sadness of their deaths. As though the overruling Providence desired that the young men of this era and of future times should study deeply the lives of Garfield and Lincoln, their deaths were made tragic to allure the student towards their chapters in the annals of society.

Looking at this man not easy to be hidden, we see the ability of our country to produce a high order of manhood. That liberty which in name has been the ideal condition of all ages here verifies all the old hopes and produces a symmetrical character strong on every side. When a lad, although poor, this Garfield enjoyed the free play of all his intellectual and emotional faculties. He was

free to move towards books and profession
and wisdom. All the gates to success would
open to him as willingly as they had opened
to a Webster or a Clay. He was not imprisoned by birth nor by caste. The path to
law or to statesmanship was as free to him as
the path along the canal, and out of this freedom of a continent came an ambition of
great power. Often when distinguished vis-
itors appear in London they are given the
freedom of the city in a gold box—an elegant letter before which the doors of galleries and libraries and parliaments and cathedrals fly open. To this youth, poor and unknown, the nation gave the freedom of the
whole circle of human acquisition, from the
study of Greek to a place in the army, from
the hall of the lawmaker to the chair of a
president ; and his ambition and energy were
inspired by the generous offer. Freedom
does not confer merit, but it affords an opportunity, and even allures the heart along
by its possible rewards. It creates a landscape which charms the eye of each one setting out upon the journey of life. Despotism offers a desert to all the humble of birth ;
if poor and of low parentage the mind sees
only an arid plain without tree or blossom :

but the liberty and equality of this land make it optional with the traveller whether the plain he is to pass over shall be a desert or a magnificent garden. All is left to personal taste and industry and will. And this taste and industry and personal power are developed by the many and great rewards offered to their growth. Mr. Garfield is one more witness in this great spiritual trial, and his testimony is direct that the liberty of America is the greatest opportunity ever offered to man as man. Elsewhere rewards are offered to the few, here all are invited to the best feast of earth.

In this eminent man the youth of to-day may learn that early poverty and hardships instead of breaking the heart need only sober the judgment and compel that common sense to come early and richly which to the children of luxury comes scantily and comes late, if ever it finds a dawn. We can now look back and perceive that the hardships in the youth of him who died as a president was only a condition of things which made all the philosophy which came to the young man assume a practical form. It was not thought a philosophy unless it held in its solution much of human happiness, for when a toiler along a canal meditates it will be for the welfare of man, just as when a slave thinks, he thinks of liberty, just as when a fever-patient dreams his dream is about cold water. It has been stated recently that the dreams and laws of reform and all welfare do not come down from the rich and great but up from the poor. Therefore those statesmen who have tasted some of the bitter things of the world know best how badly the waters need sweetening.

This patient toiler wrought out an economy for the millions of youth here and everywhere. He showed what will and industry and exalted purposes can accomplish in this wide land—that all the young need ask as an endowment is mental and physical health. That is the essential capital upon which to base a large business in things either mental or spiritual. Out of energy and taste comes the real dignity of man. This dead president carries us back to the theory of old Plato, that motion or energy lies at the origin of the universe, that the starry skies and the variegated earth are only expressions of the self-moved mind. To this notion this one heart brings us back, for out of its self-moved depths there issued a moral world of great attractiveness. Education, learning, religion, politics, duty, honour and high office emerged from the mind which began its career far down in weakness. That force made all the humble days and years to be the rich veins of the later silver and gold. As in the theology of nature we gather up the infinite phenomena of land and sea and sky and say the One mind made all these wonderful and beautiful things, so in reading this biography whose last page has just been written in tears, the reader will say, Behold what goodness and greatness have moved out of that one heart in royal pageantry!

Was James A. Garfield great? Ask those early years, when adverse winds always assailed his bark; ask the nights of study; ask the schools where he taught; ask the place where he worshipped; ask the halls where he helped enact wise laws; ask the battlefields where he led soldiers; ask the magnificent Capitol where he was crowned as republicans crown their chieftains; ask the cottage where he died. If out of the answers to these questions there comes not the witness of greatness the human heart must henceforth toil and long in vain; earth has no greatness. And yet all this human excellence grew up out of our national resources as though to show the world the peculiar richness of the soil. And grew inland so far that we cannot say that England or Europe combined with America to cause this character. The boy and man lived in the heart of the continent all surrounded by his country; and he lies in his coffin to-day a dead child of his nation. The country mourns to-day not only because a man has died, and died unjustly, and painfully, but also because that man was her son. She had reared him, she saw her own likeness in his face, she loved him; in him were a mother's hopes. This land herein shows not only the power of its institutions to fashion a noble character, but that power of appreciation and grief that can weep for one thus overtaken by death.

In the scene of these few days we must mark some signs of a higher civilization and a more sensitive brotherhood. Looking at the assassin we might despair of the present and the future. We might wonder what is the value of schoolhouse and church and literature and freedom and the eloquence over human rights if out of these beautiful things there can stalk a man much more cruel than a brute. But while the heart wonders and sinks over the name of that one savage it is cheered by seeing a whole civilized race moved by a divine pity. One vile human creature wished to remove Garfield from life, but millions upon millions wished him to live, live happily and live long. Men of wealth and men of poverty, men of learning and men of scanty education, men of all the political parties, men in the South and men in the North, and the crowned kings and queens loved the life of this one man and would by their esteem have carried him beyond the common threescore years of pilgrimage. His death was desired by the lowest one of the human race; it is lamented by the entire population of two continents. If we count or measure these tears, if we see the Queen of England ordering her court to put on the emblems of mourning, we cannot but conclude that the hate of the one assassin is sublimely outweighed by the esteem of the world. In presence of such an uprising of brotherly esteem the murderer finds his proper depth of infamy. In the light of a universal love we see the dark cruelty of the crime.

But we must not forget that we have assembled to-day in the name of the weekly service of God. If in this life of a president any quality of Christianity is placed upon a mountain top that quality cannot remain hidden. In our times when there is threatened an eclipse of faith all religious minds must be happy to recognize the public man who in his best manhood saw the power of a belief in God. He realized the perfect grandeur of the words "The Lord reigns." He uttered them in an hour of great national darkness, and the populace needed no other eloquence; and when in July last the one who had offered consolation in calamity needed some refuge for himself he said he was ready to die or to live. Not the details of any church faith came, but the great ideas of the Christian religion grouped themselves around his bed— the best angels of those sad nights, for they were to help him when the skill of man should fail.

It would be unjust to the name of Christ to say that Mr. Garfield's religion was only that of nature, only such general thoughts as were cherished by Greek and Roman pagans. His faith came to him through the church of the age as it communicates its ideas through pulpit and press and the Testament, as it is wont to surround and teach the young all through the days of formation, of passion and temptation. That church encompassed this youth with its hymns and morals and trust and hope, and if at last the world saw evidences of that honour so conspicuous in the Sermon on the Mount and that belief in heaven so visible in Jesus Christ it is under some obligation to confess that Christianity helped form that character which to-day all admire and lament. Beyond doubt daily association with learned men of all the different religious sects, and the daily discovery that many creeds made only one kind of religious manhood, turned Mr. Garfield away from the distinctive doctrines of a denomination and led him into the concord of faith rather than into its discord; but in estimating the greatness of his character we must declare that his moral symmetry was Christlike, and Christlike his repose in the hope of a second life. From his official and personal height he reminds the whole land that there should be church doors open to all the youth, inviting them away from the sins of the street and from the freezing touch of a godless air; there should be a Sunday secured to the young and old, that there might be some hours of sunlight for those delicate plants—faith and spirituality. If our Nation, destined in a generation more to surpass all upon the globe in power, material and mental, desires to be governed by able and good men it must see to it that the schoolhouse, and the church with its day of rest, are kept open, for through these the young pass on their way to all great beauty of character and usefulness of life.

It has been the reproach of our country that it is not rich in history; that the mind must look beyond the ocean or travel beyond the ocean to reach the presence of all that is deemed impressive. We have no venerable architecture, no historic church, no places of fame, no throne-rooms or prisons or towers or crowns or jewels made affecting by the annals of a thousand years. This objection to our new world is well made; but this poverty of our country is being rapidly exchanged for riches—the riches seen in such men as Lincoln and Garfield and similar moral products of the Republic. A nation will not long remain without history when the lives of such men are rapidly entering into the great open page. The old world in its thousand-year period, reaching from the Twelfth Century to the Nineteenth, cannot point us to better names—names which stand for a better union of intelligence and ability and integrity and charity and heroism. Old history can point us to violent deaths of rulers, and can say here Charles I was beheaded; here Mary of the Scots died; here Marat was slain; but our two great presidents have been slain not by a multitude which was wronged but by private fanatics, in their attack as unauthorized as beasts of prey. While old history abounds in instances where men died for some sins or wrongs, our new history points us to two great leaders who were the unhappy victims each of a single wicked heart; and died to gratify no party but amid the tears of all parties and factions of the land.

Rapidly is our country making up a history which will surpass those books we all read in our early years. It cannot be affirmed of many of those illustrious ones whose names besprinkle the records of human life that they surpassed this Garfield in the power to measure the wants of society and in the sympathy that cannot forget the welfare of the people. Where ancient great men trampled about in the living fields, this man walked softly, fear-ing lest some flower might be crushed. That attachment to the aged mother, that measureless attachment to the wife, were only evidences that this President was the type and product of a new age which was putting aside ferocity and was reaching a sensibility as to human rights which was not present in the men who ruled once those nations which now boast of possessing history. The American pages may not be many, but comparatively they are white.

Must we not to-day read anew the lesson of mortality ? Must not we who have come into this church from the many paths of the world, along which paths we too are allured by some one of the many forms of ambition and hope, feel deeply the undeniable fact that we are all hastening to the end ? The closing scene may not be tragic, but it is coming. We are asked to think of these things by the memory of both Lincoln and Garfield, for they were both half-melancholy men, the former loving pathetic poetry, the latter even writing it. Lincoln in the height of his fame would say :

" The hand of the king that the sceptre hath borne,
  The brow of the priest that the mitre hath worn,
  The eye of the sage and the heart of the brave,
  Are hidden and lost in the depths of the grave.

" The peasant whose lot was to sow and to reap,
  The herdsman who climbed with his goats up the steep,
  The beggar who wandered in search of his bread,
  Have faded away like the grass that we tread.''

And Garfield in the height of his success looked upon the earth of his triumph with sad eyes. He was unable to forget that he and all he loved were being borne along by arms mysterious and powerful. All sensitive minds are pathetic and almost superstitious in their hours of meditation. The dictates of reason are not able to counteract fully the deep attachments of the heart to life and friends and all the loved ones. When the great are warm-hearted they are melancholy and most plaintive. May you all possess such a pathetic estimate of our earth; may you all see the tombward march of man, so read the vanity of riches and fame and home and love, that you shall be compelled to become children of God and of Jesus Christ,—thus, children of the final country that knows no funeral pageants, no days of bitter disappointment.

IV

CHARLES SUMNER [1]

THE world has always loved to speak of
the Infinite One as being the " God of
Nations," because there is a greatness involved
in the idea of Nation which makes it seem
worthy of the attention and love of the Infinite. It is easy for the individual heart,
possessed of ordinary humility, to feel quite
overlooked in the daily administrations of
Providence, but a nation is something so
vast in its interests and in its life which lies
over centuries, that into its great events men
can generally see descending, in love or
wrath, the sublime form of God. Notwith-
standing the most elaborate and conclusive
argument that our Heavenly Father is in all
places and times alike, yet we all go away
from the argument to confess Him sooner at
Waterloo than where a child is playing or a
bird singing; more visible where slaves are
shouting in a new liberty than where a
farmer turns his furrow or the lonely wood-

[1] Died March 11, 1874.

man swings his axe. Thus marking the
habits of the human mind, we may perceive
at least how great a thing is a nation. What
a vast idea it is, that it always claims the
care of the Almighty, and almost compels
the atheist to confess that there is at least a
nation's God.

A nation is a second world into which we
are all born. The first world is only the
good green earth, with its seasons, and food,
and labour, and natural vicissitudes; but
this is a poor birthplace for a mind or a
soul, for into these poor, brutish arms falls
the Indian child or the young Arab. To be
born into earth alone is a fate that robs a
birthday of all worth. It is only an animal
that is born to earth alone. It is only when
some second world called a "nation" becomes the soul's cradle that it becomes desirable to fall heir to life. A nation is a
grand equipment for a career; it is food,
and clothes, and friends first, and education,
and employment, and culture, and religion
afterwards. It is the atmosphere into which
the many-winged spirit comes; and a bird
might as well spread its wings in a vacuum
as for a human soul to be born away from
the treasured-up virtues of a national life.

When the rude black face, with retreating forehead and great thick lips, meets you on the Southern coast, you know that that being was born, but you associate with this knowledge the other fact that he was born to savage Africa. Great beyond all estimate, therefore, is the fact of *nation*, for it shapes the soul, and is the joy or sorrow of every being that comes into this existence. As when, in the setting sun, after a summer shower, all things, clouds, hills, trees, and even the very grass and the faces of our friends standing in the refracted light are covered with the tinge of gold, so when man is born into a nation he is instantly bathed in its light, and sets forth in a double destiny, that of man and that of citizen; and it is, for the most part, the latter destiny that determines the value of life. When Bunyan saw a culprit ascending the steps to the gallows, he said: "That were I, but for the Grace of God;" but this Grace does not busy itself only with individuals here and there, but it marks out a vast realm and makes it a great, free, civilized state, and then the millions that come into life in its blessed confines can, in their later years, when they realize the value of the great fatherland, say, "I was a savage, a Congo negro, but for the Grace of God."

Next to the grandeur of a planet with a thousand millions of people upon its bosom, whirling them along through day and night, and summer and winter, and youth and old age, comes the grandeur of a well-equipped State which, for hundreds of years, guards the liberty, and industry, and education, and happiness of her dependent millions, crowding her influence in upon them gently as the atmosphere lies upon the cheek in June. Her language, her peculiar genius, her ideals, her religion, her freedom, enwrap us better than our mother's arms, for the State enwraps her too, and wreathes her forehead with a merit that warrants her office and her affection. The State is defined to be a

> "   .   .   .   Sovereign law, that with collected will,
> Sits Empress, crowning good, repressing ill.
> Smit by her sacred frown
> The fiend Dissension like a vapour sinks
> And e'en the all dazzling Crown
> Hides his faint rays and at her bidding shrinks."

Whence comes this grand instrument which, as now existing in our continent, under the flag of liberty, pours around forty millions of people such a golden air as

no millions ever breathed before ? Who
gathered these flowers that wreathe equally
our cradle, our altar, our homes, and our
whole earthly pilgrimage ? This much of a
reply is given by human experience : Nothing comes to man, of excellence, without
labour. All that man possesses of art, science, or literature, or invention, has come by
regular payments made in hard toil. As the
verdure that waves over the whole earth has
come from the daily sacrifice of the sun's
heat, so the glory manifold of each great
nation has come by the path of human sacrifice of thought, and toil, and even life ; and
so valuable have been the national ideas,
that, for all the good the world possesses,
there have been fields baptized with the
heart's best blood. Young though many of
the modern free nations may be in their
present name and form, yet back of each
one lie a thousand years of active labour, and
often of deep agony. As geologists now tell
us that before God fitted up this earth for
man, while the mists were rising from its
heated seas, and condensing in the cooler
upper air, there were often awful storms
where the thunder rolled incessantly for a
hundred years ; so each nation which we see

standing forth now in peace and beauty—
England, Germany, America—has emerged
from a thousand-year storm, where the wrath
of man has rolled in thunder for centuries,
and the cruel skies have rained blood. One
of the poets says:

" A thousand years scarce serve to form a state."

And oh! what years of toil and vicissitude
they are to the brains which stand at the
throne, and to the hearts that stand in the
battle, and to the widow and orphan who
weep when the smoke rolls away and reveals
the dead!

If then a great nation like our own has
come over a two-thousand-year path under a
sky of alternate peace and storm, come along
from free Athens, and free Rome and sacred
Palestine, there must have been all along
guardian angels of its long journey, glorious
leaders of its wilderness march; souls that
smote rocks for its thirsty multitudes, and
prayed down manna in the still night. The
morals of our day can look back and see
their Seneca, their Confucius, but chiefly
their Divine Jesus; the art of our era looks
back and beholds its Phidias, its Apelles, its
Angelo, linking the future and the past;

poetry and all literature look back and cast
smiles of gratitude to Homer and Thucydides
and Dante; the law confesses the deep
devotion of Cicero and Justinian as minds
who studied justice when the world seemed
young.

And now, beholding this differentiation of
men by a wise providence of God, so that
each part of the soul's vast vineyard may
have some one to love its vines, we reach
the easy conclusion that the same wisdom
will permit us always to hold in memory and
in love men who, turning aside from other
pursuits, have found in the study and love
and service of their nation their own special
path between the cradle and the grave. It
is a blessed thought that there have risen up
here and there not only hearts that could
weave the sweet songs of a Virgil, and not
only hands that could paint the pictures of a
Parrhasius, or that could strike the notes of
a Mozart; not only minds that may throw
up a dome of St. Peter's, or that may as-
tonish the world with their invention, but
also other hearts which have loved the idea
of Nation, and have lived and died not in the
arms of a friend, but rather in the arms of
the country. Out of the thoughts and love

and specialization of these great ones we, humbler children of the State, have all drawn our happiness and freedom, as the violets are invited into life by the all-loving sun.

In the week past the grave has opened suddenly and taken back one of these souls which seem sent of God to know nothing else but their country, as Paul knew nothing else but the Cross. Into that tomb which grows wider each year and has received away from our sight Washington and the Adamses and Jefferson and Clay and Webster and Lincoln, at last has been gathered one more name wreathed as heavily as any with the glorious ideas and honours of our great Republic. Napoleon loved not a nation, but his own power. He was a student not of justice, but of crowns; he studied how to destroy other diadems, and of their jewels weave one for himself.

> " The triumph and the vanity,
>   The rapture of the strife,
> The earthquake voice of victory,
>   To thee the breath of life ;
> The sword, the sceptre, and that sway,
>   Which man seemed made but to obey,
> Wherewith renown was rife,
>   All quell'd ! Dark Spirit, what must be
> The madness of thy memory ! "

But the memory of that life just ended has no madness in it, but is all a remembrance of honour, and charity, and peace.

It seems especially fitting the day and place that we should devote this hour to thoughts over this fresh tomb, for the greatness of Mr. Sumner's career is strangely interwoven with some of the noblest ideas of Christianity; and this union was not accidental, nor prudential, but spiritual and intellectual, for Mr. Sumner in his life, devoted to humanity, so framed all his arguments, and so based them upon the philosophy of Christ that the perpetual return of the terms Christianity and Saviour betrays the fact that much of his eloquence was only the Sermon upon the Mount applied, not to the future of the soul, but to the true, earthly progress of mankind. If any group of philosophers were to sit down with the Life of Christ in their hands, with the desire to elaborate a political constitution from its pages, among the many principles they would bring forth we should at once certainly find these—peace, justice, and equality. From justice would instantly come liberty. Now of that eventful life whose untimely ending drapes this day with sorrow, these three Christian ideas, peace, liberty, and equality, were the opening and final strain, the matin and the vesper. The public career of Mr. Sumner began by that unrivalled oration spoken thirty years ago upon peace as the source of national grandeur; and without any deviation, any faltering along this path, he is found at last on the border of death, asking Congress not to paint upon its flags of the present and future the names of battles where brothers fought. His life was all set to one music, and it was a heavenly strain without discord.

But before I ask you to think of those three great ideas, in which Mr. Sumner did great service for the Christianity out of which he took the ideas, and the Christlike spirit, too, permit me to apologize, so far as it may be necessary, for the marble coldness which has long been associated with this eminent character. Let us empty our minds of this prejudice. A public man, writing a private letter since the death of this senator, says: "He was cold as a statue. He was a child of principles and books, and consequently had little in common with the humanities of life. . . . I cannot speak of him generally in this regard; but in the few times in which I dined with him at Mr. Lincoln's table, he

was a pleasant dinner companion, and con-
versed happily and instructively; but such
times were only little outbreaks of sunlight.
In the main, he was behind the cloud, and,
while full of gentle humanity, he moved
among individuals evolving an austere sense
of superiority." Against the truth of these
statements from one who had the opportunity
and the discrimination for reading well the
qualities of this distinguished man, we would
say nothing; indeed, the portraiture just
given may be confessed to be sufficiently
correct. But that he was capable of deep
friendship is fully seen in his attachment to
the loved President, whose house was so dear
to him that he repaired there daily as to a
sacred home where he loved all and was also
deeply loved.

Passing by this inquiry, I only wish to
remind you that all the great intellectual
development which the world has ever seen
has been reached at the cost of the heart.
" Where the treasure is," says the Bible,
" there the heart will be also "; and hence,
when an old scholar of the dark ages found
his love of thought increasing, he began to
withdraw from the streets, and to find, in
some monastic cell, all of the world that any

longer remained in his heart; and although the dark ages are gone, and the monasteries are dust, yet the principle remains that, when the intellect weds itself fully to certain paths of study and toil, the heart soon sunders the other many sweet and beautiful associations of the wide world, and casts its love upon that realm only to which the intellect may have wedded itself for better or for worse, for richer or poorer. It is an unconscious sacrifice which genius is always compelled to make; but it is no more visible over the grave of Sumner than over the grave of Mill in philosophy, or Pascal in metaphysics, or Angelo in art, or Cicero in law and letters. It is written in all history that a life of thought is a constant warfare against a life of sociability and cheerfulness and love. Instead of recalling the marble coldness of past illustrious men as a blemish or a fault in their character, we only indicate a common fact, and we would bury the defect forever under offerings of gratitude, that there have come here and there souls which, for the development of great, useful ideas, have been able to abandon what we mortals in a humbler vale call the varied pleasures of life. But they have not so much lost happiness as exchanged that of sense for that of spirit.

Turning aside now from this apology, let us rejoice that if it was the fate of the lamented senator to live for only a part of earth and for only a part of religion, that it pleased him to live for so magnificent a part of both politics and religion as is found in the words peace, justice, and liberty.

It was not Mr. Sumner, you remember, who advised the partnership of Bibles and rifles in the early days of Kansas. No, in all this forty years of public life, Mr. Sumner stood by the power of argument, of light, of Christian civilization alone. His hymn was the poet's psalm of peace :

" Were half the power that fills the world with terror,
    Were half the wealth bestowed on camps and courts,
Given to redeem the human mind from error,
    There were no need of arsenals or forts.

" The warrior's name would be a name abhorred,
    And every nation that should lift again
Its hand against a brother, on its forehead
    Would wear, forever more, the curse of Cain."

In the pulpits of the whole land the Gospel doctrines had, for the most part, been applied to only individual welfare, and chiefly to

that welfare beyond the confines of states—
beyond the grave. Afraid, for the most
part, to preach what they called politics;
and having, to an alarming extent, such a
bad politics that it was perhaps fortunate
that they remained silent even by a theological mistake, the Christian ministry had,
in the last generations, left the gospel of
nations to be preached by the few disciples
of William Penn and by such virtual Quakers
as Channing and Whittier, and Sumner, the
greatest of all. Upon him there was no
restraint. No false creed, no temporary
policy such as influenced Webster and Clay,
no fear of violence, no fear of public scorn,
either from Boston or New Orleans, ever
held him in any conceivable chain, but from
him, the freest man our country ever had in
its dark days, came the gospel of nations in
all its Bethlehem beauty of truth and spirit.
In the present, and more yet, in the near and
far future, the pulpit will confess that
Charles Sumner was a minister at its altar
in dark days when it was afraid, and in doctrines to the grandeur of which it had not
the intellect, nor the courage, nor the humanity to ascend. Penn and Channing and
Sumner came in with that part of Christian-

ity which belongs to the constitution of nations; and when we remember that a grand,
free, enlightened State is the land in which
the Cross can ever be reared with most success, the orators who, upon the field of
statesmanship, apply to society the three
Christian doctrines of peace, liberty and
justice, must be confessed to be standing
very near the holiest ministers of religion.
As the church helped Mr. Sumner, gave him
hearts willing to listen to his long argument,
so he helped the church by sending back to
it men who evermore tried to combine the
character of Christian with the character of
citizen.

But Mr. Sumner's attachment to peace was
no more absorbing and unbending than his
devotion to liberty. For liberty is twin
sister of peace, as bondage is the companion
of violence. As Franklin gloried in saying
"Where liberty is there is my country,"
Sumner equally gloried in saying "Where
liberty is there is my party." Down this
channel of freedom, for white slaves in
Barbary, and for black slaves in America, he
poured a torrent of eloquence for twenty-five
years, a stream of argument, which gathering
up the wisdom of Greece and Rome, the ex·

perience of England, the battle-shouts of
Marathon and Bunker Hill, the blest vision
of all the poets, the longings of Washington
and Jefferson, and then bedecking the stream
with flowers of a gorgeous rhetoric growing
upon either bank, moved along like an
Amazon towards the sea. It has been said
recently by a public man, that Mr. Sumner
"surpassed all statesmen in the love and
study of the right." It was this deep pre-
possession that led him to espouse the cause
of the slave. Words which he himself applied
to Channing thirty years ago return now to
settle upon his own forehead. "Follow my
white plume," said the chivalrous monarch
of France. *Follow the right*, more resplendent than plume or oriflamme, was the watchword of Sumner. But all this long history
you know well, for in this hour when death
has come to quicken our memory and love,
an hour which makes an enemy a friend, all
that past struggle for the slave's freedom, and
the discord of the Missouri Compromise down
to the death of Mr. Lincoln, a tragedy which
closed the long, awful drama, flashes through
your hearts with no detail of sadness left out.
Recall the great pageant and see this white
face above the common mortals.

But to-day, we can only turn aside from the usual themes of the sacred desk to bless the heavenly Father for this child that came in the name of that form of civilization which finds its best exponent in the Saviour of mankind, and bless Him that there was one tongue which for a generation made the best eloquence of this free land beam with the light of Him whose gospel is not only a perfect salvation, but a perfect civilization,—the vital air, not only of a saint, but of a citizen. And we cannot close these thoughts without asking you to read in this urn of perishable dust, but of imperishable memory, a lesson of hope which may serve us all in coming days, perhaps of the country, but surely of our own heart. When government, and pulpit, and press were voiceless and hopeless as to a time when the Nation's flag should be freed from its last reproach, this mental sight which is closed now saw plainly in the future a day when all the States would be free, and when the national banner would proclaim liberty and justice wherever it should wave. His was a hopefulness which nothing but death could abate; and blest with such a prophetic, almost inspired sense, he, in all the years of our civil war, was calm, and was to Mr.

Lincoln, upon whose mind and heart a burden rested which would have wearied an Atlas accustomed to uphold the globe, a daily messenger of faith and hope in both man and God. Perhaps the marble-like nature of the statesman was a peace and strength to a president whose heart was always full of tenderness and melancholy strangely mingled. That immense power of hope which has always attended men of ideals, the angel of their need, accompanied Mr. Sumner in all hours, and held him up far above the discord of the passing time. A poem which he greatly loved shows us what kind of a hymn sounded in the sky over his daily toil. It inspired him in the night watches:

> " There's a fount about to stream,
>   There's a light about to beam,
>   There's a warmth about to glow,
>   There's a flower about to blow.
>   There's a midnight blackness changing
>   Into gray ;
>   Men of thought and men of action,
>   Clear the way ! "

Oh! why may not the pulpit and each Christian rise to this calm atmosphere of a trust in God, and as this statesman always saw liberty and justice about to come down

out of God's sky, why may not the soldier of
the cross daily say to his soul

     "There's a fount about to stream,
      There's a light about to beam,"

and live in this magnificent hope?

But our time has passed. Much of our
country's mental and moral glory has gone
down in past years. We seem to have
only an evening horizon into which golden
suns sink, but from which none arise. The
melancholy gate of death by which these
souls depart seems wider than the gates of
life by which such glorious beings are marching towards our bereaved hearts. Yet this
apparent triumph of the grave may come
from the fact that we can see the past in all
its desolation, but cannot unveil the future
and see its compensating good. We can only
hope that the gates of God's mercy are as
wide as the gates of His death, and that the
solemn West into which these lights are sinking from our sky may, by its shadows,
remind us that there is an Eastern heaven
radiant with divine love, upon whose bosom
other orbs will appear, resplendent with
peace, justice, and liberty.

V

WENDELL PHILLIPS [1]

A S these deaths of the great occur, they
become more and more painful, because the group of heroes grows smaller, and
the loss of one more great soul is the more
deeply felt. It has not been many years since
our Nation was rich in the style of manhood
represented by him who has just been buried.
We could see, not long ago, Chase and Parker, Sumner and Henry Wilson and Lincoln
and Greeley and Gerrit Smith and Garrison,
and others of similar power ; but as the years
have gone by, these have gone with them, and
so small at last has the group become, that
upon each new invasion of death, we all wonder if any one remains to be a golden link
between the present and the past. So rapidly
do these noble chieftains fall into the tomb
that many of the young minds of to-day will
never see any one of these noble faces, but
will be compelled to find their souls only in

[1] Died February 2, 1884.

history. Those of you who have seen and heard all these great Americans, from Webster to Phillips, may well be proud now of such a memory. They surpassed the sculptor and painter and poet and musician, for while those artists give us the decorations and pleasures of life, these statesmen helped lay the foundations of liberty, and hence of all that leans upon liberty for support. Art, education, commerce, industry, science, and religion, have drawn life from these master-builders in the political temple. Angelo and Raphael in art are outdone by these pioneers in the career of our republic. Art comes only to a few; a great country empties her blessings upon all the millions, and what blessings they are!

A religious, political mind like that of Wendell Phillips possesses in the formative years of a nation a worth we can with difficulty measure; certainly we cannot rate it at too high a price. In 1836 this man, then fresh from the schools and college, and with a mind blessed far beyond the lot of common mortals, turned aside from profession and traffic, to give his hand and heart to one single cause, the emancipation of his country's slaves. From 1836 to 1863, that is, for

twenty-seven years, he turned the river of
his eloquence down through that barren and
dangerous plain. For not many men of
even Boston birth and culture touched foot
in that day upon the land of negro freedom.
It was like the forest that lay before Dante
in his dream, full of wild, ravenous beasts—
the wolf of avarice, the leopard of sin, the
lion of power. The merchants were influenced by the wolf of avarice, the fashionable people by the leopard of sin, the poli-
ticians by the lion of power. Dante, in presence of these beasts, determined to rise
above them and dream of, and visit heaven.
So Phillips, in his glory of youth and genius,
resolved to rise above all these destroyers
and find those heights where no wild beast
has a lair—heights towards the throne of
peace and right. To have made such a
choice seems easy now, but had this entire
audience been citizens of Boston at that
date, it may be that no one of us would have
offered hand or heart to the pleading slave.
The tide of New England sentiment flowed
towards the cotton which grew at the bid-
ding of the slave; and to touch slavery was
assumed the same as making the grass to
grow in the manufacturing streets. Thus an

Abolitionist was deemed an enemy of the land once occupied by the Puritans.

When, in about 1840, some one became bold enough to bring Frederick Douglass into Boston to preach in a prominent church upon the condition and rights of the slaves, no one dared to invite him home to dinner after the morning service; but all left the eloquent ex-slave to pass the afternoon among the tombstones in the churchyard— perhaps stones in memory of those who had sailed from Europe or England to establish liberty. It was at such a time of bondage to commerce and manufactures and of cruelty towards man, that Mr. Phillips made the vow of consecration to the cause of freedom.

Our country thus suffers the loss of one who, born in the highest rank of society, declined its luxury and exclusiveness, and, Christlike, went down to the humble world of the African to be his friend. It was an immense gain for the general cause of humanity; for not only came thus to that cause a warm heart and a brave soul, but there came the finest orator of the century—a mind as calm as the blue sky, as fascinating as the summer time, and yet as powerful as the earthquakes and torrents and tempests.

Very often the poor of earth have had to accept of the services of some man whose mind was untrained, whose reason was weak, whose judgment was quick and ill founded, whose information small, but such was not the misfortune of our African millions in their later years. There came to their aid the best sons the world could produce— Theodore Parker, Horace Mann, Thomas Starr King, Charles Sumner and Wendell Phillips. From such brains and souls there poured forth for twenty-five years a stream of matchless eloquence which prepared the Nation for that day when ideas would be compelled to make a final struggle upon the battle-field. In the first years of the liberty movement the slave had few friends in the North, but what he had were of rare quality. Slavery held the trade of New England ; freedom gradually won her intellect and heart ; slavery held the cotton-mill, freedom the library ; slavery was represented by a policeman with a metallic star on his breast and a club in his hand ; freedom was represented by an orator whose forehead was as proud as that of Apollo and whose lips were like those of Pericles ; the ship-load of cotton from the Georgia plantations became at last less valuable than the divine philosophy upon New England soil, and in the sharp conflict between merchant and orator the orator won.

Gone are all those days of mingled light and darkness, hope and fear, great virtues and great sins, but this recent death has re-called the past, and may well awaken in our bosoms gratitude to God that He gave to our Nation the men needed in its successive hours. We should be dull and ungrateful children should we not see the many-coloured glory of those past years and realize that He who planted flowers and made the ocean and the stars is the One who created oratory out of the dust and clothed it also with beauty and power. Oratory is the universe bursting out into speech.

It is not a pertinent inquiry whether Mr. Phillips might not have accomplished more for the times had he harmonized more with the local and central Government and had he been more closely allied to senates and cabinets. Such questions belong rather to some shop of biography or history. Two thoughts in that matter will suffice us to-day; the one, that his life as it stands was so full of the true and good that we should seem greedy beggars should we demand more. To

come along with our perfect ideal of a statesman or a philanthropist, and to set about
comparing our golden and divine mask with
this dead human face would be only an illus-
tration of our meanness and injustice. Instead of coming forward with our portrait
painted after the fact, after the long battle
and the death, we should rather come with
the wonder what heroism or perfection we
would have shown had we lived in that New
England city while those times of dull conscience and bridled tongue were passing
slowly by. Nor can we determine now just
how great a crime it was not to vote at the
elections nor seek the duties of a government
which could open its new Territories to the
system of slavery, and which could compel a
Northern man to help capture and return a
fugitive from bondage. So difficult are these
problems that we may well thank God for
what of pure truth and nobleness there came
into the Nation's mind from these now word-
less lips. Their eloquence was at least of
grand quality, as powerful and beautiful as
it was useful.

The second apologetic thought is this—
that no age calls for men of similar mental
and emotional structure, for men who will

all vote and seek and hold office and blend
into one common picture. In the whole
history of our race there has been a constant
call for a variety which would not permit
any two leaders to resemble each other.
Hence biographers can with difficulty find
parallels. They attempt to find some resemblance between Dante and Milton, or Savonarola and Luther, Burke and Webster, but
after rhetoric and research have toiled hard
at the comparison, there stands on the one
hand Savonarola, and on the other Luther,
with a measureless and mysterious space between. Nature never repeats any form of
greatness. Plato was not Socrates, Virgil
was not Homer, Washington was not Crom-
well, Wendell Phillips was not Abraham
Lincoln. Thus moves onward the vast
human race, lifting up its vast sons in her
loving arms, but with no duplicate ever of
face, or brain, or heart. And thus did the
march of events train and inform and call
and adopt and employ for a lifetime this
man now of world-wide fame. His age created him for its special service.

Nothing more loudly proclaims the being
of a God than His perpetual procession of
such gifted mortals. Look at a single group

of them as springing up in one single city; Everett, Webster, Sumner, Longfellow, Emerson, and in all a large assemblage of titanic brothers, able by joining hands to move the world. And to that one city add other places on our globe, where man has unfolded his power, places between London and old Athens; add names from Pitt to Demosthenes, and what holy ground our earth becomes! We forget the sins and follies of the common millions, and pass easily from these giants in mind and morals to the presence of a Creator. Listening to their spoken words or reading their volumes, we realize at once the grandeur of man, the divineness of his exploits, and the probable glory of his final destiny. While near the common roaring of wheels, or while amid the perishable decorations of fashion, or in the midst of its vivacity and laughter, man may seem an ephemeral insect, but the scene all changes when we meet the great in their ordained paths, their forms seem larger than life, and their faces seem to contain some mysterious proofs of immortality.

When Wendell Phillips began his public life evangelical Christianity did not look upon him as an ally. It was thought that

such orators as Parker and Phillips would
lead thousands to spiritual ruin, and some
clergymen even prayed that Providence
might remove Theodore Parker from this
existence. These two were counted as the
Church's enemies; but such have been the
changes in thought and argument and in the
questions of debate that no doubt the Christian world rejoices to-day when it recalls an
eloquence which founded itself upon the
being of the heavenly Father, and the presence everywhere of a "higher law." The
wit and anecdote and irony and awful
denunciation of Phillips seldom ran onward
many minutes without some appeal to the
existence and justice of God. When the tele-
graph flashed to Boston that Mr. Lincoln
had been elected and a joyous crowd assembled in Tremont Temple to hear what
Mr. Phillips would say, he closed his memorable speech by these words of new hope:
"Once plant deep in the Nation's heart the
love of right, let there grow out of it a firm
purpose of duty, and then from the higher
plane of Christian manhood we can put
aside on the right hand and left all narrow,
childish and mercenary considerations. For
us, the children of a pure civilization, the

pioneers of a Christian future, it is for us to found a capitol whose corner-stone shall be justice, whose top stone liberty; within the sacred precincts of whose Holy of Holies shall dwell One who is no respecter of persons, but hath made of one blood all the nations of the earth. Crowding to the shelter of its stately arches I see old and young, learned and ignorant, rich and poor, native and foreign, Pagan, Jew and Christian, black and white, in one glad, harmonious, triumphant procession."

In that far-off day the Church was not able to see religion where it could not see Orthodoxy, and therefore the deep Christianity of Parker and Mann and Phillips was not confessed; but in our day atheism has invaded the field of eloquence and has created a black cloud upon which the belief of Phillips bends plainly all its colours of righteousness and love and hope. All that anti-slavery which echoed through the Nation for twenty-five years was based upon the laws of the Almighty, and what confession the Church could not make while those men were living it will make at last over their graves.

In those years which lay between 1840 and 1860 the languishing minds of public men and private citizens, of preachers and writers, needed plain words, sharp and rude. It was a period of general hesitation and weakness. Into such a dead atmosphere Phillips moved with the vehemence of a storm. No man, living or dead, equals this name in the power of cutting speech, the power of statement, of citation of instance, of application, and of never bending pursuit of one end. In the hottest days of the struggle the eloquence of Wendell Phillips ran not like a mad torrent but as a deep stream of fire. It scorched what it touched of wrong and folly. It was well that not all were like him, for we needed the tenderness of Lincoln as much as this volcanic flame; but Mr. Phillips performed his part in the drama of liberty, and performed it well.

It will become an impressive picture in history,—that of this husband and wife dedicating themselves, their time and fortune to one noble enterpise; so noble that it dwarfs the common ends and aids of to-day. This work displaced their love of furniture and drapery and silks and broadcloth and fashionable life, and arose before them as sweet as the Star of Bethlehem before the wise men of the East. These two said to Liberty: "We have seen thy star and have come to worship thee," and opening their treasures of intellect and soul, they presented unto this Liberty their gold and frankincense and myrrh.

Beyond doubt Mr. Phillips made many mistakes, and was not as acute to measure the value of the Union as to feel the wrong of slavery. He could see a poor man or poor woman or child further than he could see a Nation. Demosthenes went around with his eloquence to induce the Greek states to unite; he failed, and Greece was ruined. Phillips on the opposite urged the American States to separate; he failed and the Nation was saved. But after we have estimated at their full demerit all the errors of this man, he remains the purest and strongest friend the lower classes ever possessed on this side the sea. He could not see anything except the rights of man. What the classics had recorded upon that subject, the aphorisms in the past or in the present, in Cicero or De Tocqueville, in incidents, in history, the great or wandering poems of any place or time having liberty and equality in their words or verses, sank into memory and came forth in his speeches as at Arethusa an underground river bursts forth.

But all this brilliant and lofty and cutting oratory has passed by. It was overthrown not by this new grave but by the freedom of man and by the grand reunion of the States. Thus this eloquence ended with the ending of its cause. What gratitude should fill our hearts that the Nation needs no more such an oratory of wormwood, but asks now for the literature of a brotherhood and for lives full of all noble action! Perhaps in years not far away the South herself when she shall look with pride upon her enlarged cities and industries and upon millions as rich and happy as her sky is gentle and blue, will count among her friends the name of him who once seemed such a reckless enemy. The apparent foes of to-day are often the real friends of to-morrow.

What are the inferences from this life? One is that the cause of man, which possessed such simplicity in the former generation, possesses still all that physical and spiritual worth. There is no end to this service to society. Washington's camp on the Delaware would have been in vain had it not been followed by the schoolhouse and the church on the Ohio and Mississippi and the Lakes. Thus, each step of a great man involves another step by a successor. Cicero said that a man who helps save a country is as worthy as one who founded it. Thus, merit is a golden chain of which each generation is a link. The chain falls weak and worthless when any generation makes a feeble link. The task resting upon the new men and new women—all children when Parker and Phillips were in all their glory of wrath and love—is one of the same old greatness, that of leading onward and yet onward the public, for which so many lived and died.

A second inference is one of both rhetoric and religion. The world calls Wendell Phillips eloquent. What is eloquence? A difficult question; but we may approach it by indirection. What is great music? Certainly not a dance or a waltz, because the theme or emotion is too childish. A Marseillaise hymn will illustrate great music because all that pathos and beauty of sound reposes upon the worth and history of impressive France. What is architecture? Surely not the building of a bookcase or a fireplace or a portico; but the rearing of some structure under which is some great thought, a library, a gallery, a kingdom, a worship of the Al-

mighty. The greater the idea, the greater
the architecture; hence most of the wonderful piles of earth repose upon religion—
two worlds, the one here and the one here-
after. Such thoughts may bring us near to
a definition. Eloquence is the adequate
treatment of a vast theme. The theme sends
its greatness up into the words as the falling
waters of Niagara send into the woods afar
in the still night the strange outline of their
thundering. A great mind treating a great
theme are the two elements needed to make
eloquence. In Phillips these met. In Webster they met for a time, but afterwards they
parted. They are seen joining in Burke and
Pitt. They combined in Robert Ingersoll
when he spoke in memory of the soldiers
and saw "the past rise up before him like a
dream," but they part when the same gifted
speaker discourses against the being of a
God and the hope of a second life; the great
mind runs on from hour to hour, but the
theme is wanting and there is no oratory
possible in the case. Eloquence is therefore
a great treatment of a great subject.

Phillips saw the human race all standing
together as children of God. God had made
their world; had made the soil, the seasons,

the human hand and heart and genius, had
given laws whose obedience would bring
happiness ; and from such a premise Wendell
Phillips moved outward towards the vision
of Human Liberty and Equality.   His memory bids us remember ever that glorious word,
FREEDOM.

VI

HENRY WARD BEECHER[1]

THIS is a peculiar day [March 12, 1887]. It is the first Sunday of more than fifty years whose morning has not called Mr. Beecher to the sanctuary; the first morning in which he could not obey such a blessed invitation. In a series of spring-times which, in the retrospect, seems interminable, Mr. Beecher has responded like a child to the invitations of sunshine, bird, and blossom to grasp anew God's world and man's world; he has rushed joyfully forth for more than seventy years and has extracted from the seasons colours and perfumes to be woven into his speech. This spring ends all the running out and in of that soul, and we have come upon a Sunday and a March which sing no longer any kind of carol or psalm to that heart. In those budding months, when Freedom was attempting to find a home in Kansas, this orator of the people was in our

[1] Died March 8, 1887.

124

world; in that March when Mr. Lincoln was journeying to Washington, Mr. Beecher was here, visible as the continent. It is no common event that we have now come to the end of this long, lasting and brilliant spectacle.

Mr. Beecher's greatest years were only twenty in number, lying between 1845 and 1865. That group of twenty years was made tremendous by the great ideas which lay beneath them. These great years would have been thirty had not his large themes died from fulfillment. We cannot find fault with good dreams which suddenly end by coming true. His mind and body were equal to a longer service, but England needed no longer any instruction as to America; Kansas needed no more intercession; the slaves needed no more of the eloquence of abolition. The cathedral of liberty had been completed and the architect had only to go inside and become a worshipper. For twenty years this wonderful man worked for the human race, then he wrought twenty more years for his parish, this last score of summers being also full of power, but not to be compared with the time when the toil was for the Nation, and the tasks the greatest upon earth. In the greater period he seemed under the employ of the people to plead their cause in politics and religion. His pulpit moved around in the daily press, and was on the banks of the Ohio and the Missouri, while, as the old Scottish clans sprang forth from the bushes when their chieftain gave a blast on his trumpet, the audiences of this evangelist issued at his call from all the hills of the East and the waving grass of the West. In times of deep distress the slaves' souls cried out with the Scotch poet:

> " Oh, for a blast of that dread horn,
> On Fontarabian echoes borne ! "

The public service of Daniel Webster did not cover so wide a space in time; nor did the great career of Abraham Lincoln take in so many circles of the sun; to Mr. Beecher must be given the fame and gratitude for a battle long fought, and well fought, to the final perfect triumph.

The philosophy of his history was about of this outline. He was an inborn, vast genius, so sensitive that he became Americanized easily and deeply. As Angelo under Italy and the Medici became coloured by art, as

Goethe absorbed all the sweet odours and bewildering fancy of Germany, as Shakespeare caught all of his age in his wide mental dragnet, thus Henry Ward Beecher was Americanized, and from his brain came forth an American Politics and an American Religion. These two structures arose at the same time, whether side by side, or one within the other, cannot be affirmed. You may if you choose say the new politics was the external temple, the new religion a golden altar within. It will matter little what form of figure the thought may assume, the truth remains that under the hand of this one workman there sprang up a new form of both politics and religion. The rationalism and humanity which led slaves up out of bondage could not do otherwise than lead God's children out of old Puritanism with its election, reprobation, and literal and eternal fire. For twenty years without intermission rolled forth this eloquence about justice as between man and man and as between God and man.

The son inherited from his father the disposition and the courage to become practical and do the best things for an age and in the best light of an age. Lyman Beecher came into this world for the purpose of seeing it.

His eye was never closed, his tongue never tied. His speech was clear and sharp. He found drinking whiskies and brandies a habit of even the clergy. The moment he saw this serpent's head he struck at it. The clergy had listened to it as did their weak mother, but when Lyman Beecher came along he denounced the serpent as a falsifier, and began pounding it.

A few of his words will tell us how mental qualities are transmitted sometimes from parent to child. When Henry was a little boy the father said of intemperance: "Our vices are digging the grave of our liberties and preparing to entomb our glory. We may despise admonition, but our destruction slumbereth not. The enormous consumption of ardent spirits in our land will produce neither minds nor bodies like those which are the offspring of temperance and virtue. Our constitutions, civil and religious, have lost that domestic discipline and official vigilance in magistrates which render obedience easy and habitual. Drunkards reel through the streets day after day and year after year with entire impunity." Such were the language, the clear diction, the practical gospel of the father. The son would have taken

this question of temperance had not the slave
become more conspicuous than the drunkard,
and had not the question of a temperate
Nation been overwhelmed by the question
of national existence. The father had said
" Let us have no grog-shop in the Republic ; "
the son said " Let us first have a republic."
Thus the clear stream of healing eloquence
which began in the old New England father
widened and deepened in the bosom of the
child, but it was the same river flowing for
the healing of the Nation.

When Henry was a young man studying
theology in Cincinnati in the seminary of
which his father was the theological head,
some clergyman arose in the surrounding
darkness and arraigned the father for holding and teaching heresy. The heresy lay in
teaching that the will of the natural man
possessed some freedom of choice; that
Christ's atonement offered its merits to all;
that eternal death did not come to us because
of Adam's sin. The trial was an effort to
make the Nineteenth Century conform to the
barbarian wisdom of the Fifteenth, to make
the Mississippi Valley love the asceticism of
the old desert, the fatalism of the old East.
In this trial came as a collateral issue an

opinion regarding the right of holding property in slaves. As Lyman Beecher shrunk somewhat from the old dogmas, the son doubled the emotion and fled from this old schoolism, as he himself said, "sick of the whole medley." "How I hated this abyss of whirling controversy which seemed full of all manner of evil things, with everything in it, indeed, but Christ!" When he began to preach at times across the river in Kentucky, to about thirty or forty people, some hearer said: "He was a smart young man but he harped all the time upon one thing—the sympathy of Christ." But this was the kind of harping which the Nation most needed. The slave-master needed the spirit of Christ, the slave needed Christian sympathy, the sinner needed the intercession and persuasion of Christ, the drunkard needed the Christian manhood. Thus the young clergyman's religion shaping itself in 1838 became from necessity both a religion and a politics because the greatest question in politics in those times was a religious question.

There is now a generation in active life in our land who did not see the uprising of this eminent man, and hence they cannot measure the height of his well-earned fame. Our land is not mourning for a great writer: Irving and Macaulay had more historic lore and literary grace than Mr. Beecher possessed; Longfellow more and better poetry; Lamartine and Coleridge could surpass him in describing nature; Winkelmann and Ruskin were greater in delineating merit and demerit in art. A heart or a mind of a type differing from all these immortals has found the end in death. Beecher joined the benevolence of a Wilberforce to the eloquence of a Henry Clay or a Webster; he did not have an eloquence that could express history, but an eloquence that could make it. A Macaulay could write a page, but a Beecher could help make the Nation that must fill the page. He made facts for eloquence to record.

When this influential manhood began, our Nation was divided into two very hostile sections. The South had become so alarmed regarding its peculiar property that a Northern man having a known love of liberty did not dare travel in the South. The Northern merchants were so anxious to retain the cotton and sugar trade of the South that they all frowned upon any politics which numbered freedom among its ideas, and they would mob or burn a church which contained the disciples of a Christian liberty and equality. The students in Dartmouth College mobbed free-soil speakers; the President sympathized with the students. Churches, schoolhouses, asylums, and homes of coloured people in the North were burned to check the spread of hope among the Africans in the South. Twelve buildings were burned in New York; one large church and many homes in Cincinnati; forty houses and two churches in Philadelphia. Pennsylvania Hall, built for anti-slavery meetings, was burned down, along with its valuable library, while Mayor and Council offered no protection and no word of sympathy. White men were imprisoned in Boston for preaching Abolitionism. In 1837 a slave had been burned to death over a slow fire in St. Louis, and for denouncing such atrocity the Rev. Elijah P. Lovejoy, of this State [Illinois], was mobbed to death.

It was in such days, reaching from 1830 to 1860, that the hot oratory of Mr. Beecher was fabricated like the bolts of Jupiter in the infernal shop of Vulcan. Thence came also the equipment of Dr. Cheever, Phillips, Parker and Sumner. The age sharpened their speech, condensed their style, and poured in the heroism and passion which make martyrs. Of all these men Mr. Beecher was the most visible, because his pulpit brought him each week before the people. His logic, his simple style, his illustrations, his pathos, his hope, made his words fly straight as arrows to the heart. This vast plea for universal freedom was well sustained for twenty years, and beginning in our West it reached its zenith in England, when, in 1863, he had to teach the horrors of slavery to the nation which had produced Cowper and Wilberforce, but had forgotten them. He embodied the new genius of the United States. He lived in 1840 the life our Nation reached thirty years afterwards. Boston railways built a mean, plain car for negroes to ride in. It was called the "Jim Crow" car. Charles Lennox Redmond, an educated coloured man, entertained in England by persons of rank and fame, and commissioned by O'Connell and Father Mathew to bear greetings from liberty in England to liberty in America, found on going from Boston to Salem, his home, that he must not take a good car, but must ride in the "Jim Crow" car. In such a time Mr. Beecher began to ask the coloured man to sit on his platform and in his church, and thus the "negro car" was met in equity by the refuge of the greatest pulpit the world possessed.

In 1835, while Mr. Beecher was looking out of his soul window with his powerful vision and tender nature, he saw in the *Charleston Courier* a notice of a public sale of slaves to satisfy a mortgage held by the Presbyterian Theological Seminary of South Carolina; he read also that the estate of the Rev. Dr. Furman was to be sold at auction— "the farm, a large theological library, twenty-seven negroes, some of them very prime, two mules, one horse, and an old wagon." In those days the Episcopal Bishop of Virginia, Dr. Meade, had published some sermons to slaves. One great thought was that they must bear well correction, and even if corrected when not guilty of the offense, they must bear the flogging in meekness and assign the whipping to some other transgression which had been concealed from these masters in the Lord.

It was high time for religion to reach out its hand to the slave. Oh, the joy our hearts should all feel that these sad facts are all so far back of us that they must be sought for in the records of almost forgotten history!

The slave block, the whip, and the slave are gone from our land forever !

Thus, if the new generation would make a true estimate of the public man who has just died, it must reproduce the scene which surrounded that preacher when his mind and heart were first espousing the cause of man and Christ. All wonder will then cease that his religion became simply that of Christ, and that his style admitted of no obscurity and no cowardice. His mind, one of the greatest ever made, came to an age which asked for simplicity, for logic, for only practical doctrine, for infinite sympathy and fearlessness. Mr. Beecher had these things to give, and he accepted the call from that period. He did not perform all the enlightened toil of the day, but he performed a tremendous work, and now, when his grave is made in a Nation which is a unit, a Nation dedicated indeed to Liberty, a Nation whose South is pressing on towards industry, wealth, and education—a Republic whose name is now respected by every throne and every cottage—that grave ought to catch from the whole country mingled flowers and tears.

These great years terminated with the triumph of freedom. In that long reach of

time made long by the fullness of thrilling
events, this pulpit orator had helped to re-
model the world's sermon, its gospel and its
politics. He had made the sermon less me-
chanical, less dry, less narrow, less mournful,
more human, more sympathetic, more orna-
mental, more able to compete with the
worldly literature of the present. He opened
up the theology of the past and took out much
superstition and filled the vacancy with
reason; he plucked out sectarianism and
inserted brotherhood; he extracted a large
part of hell and filled the vacancy with
heaven. If some errors of judgment lie
scattered over this long life they do not ruin
the landscape any more than the personal
errors of General Grant ruined his campaign
for the salvation of our country. A great
river always carries some driftwood upon its
bosom. If Mr. Beecher, in his ardour of logic
and battle, sometimes went beyond the true
boundary of doctrinal reform, it matters little,
for the new pulpit learned from its founder
the independence of thought which can
reject as readily as accept. If this Brooklyn
pulpit pencilled some new outlines of religion
and of its sermon and drew them grandly,
the pulpit of to-day must not ask him for all

the details to be put into the new discourse.
If he helped make for us a country reaching
in beauty from one sea to another, we should
not ask him to plough over fields for us and
tell us what grains and flowers to plant.
If heaven sends an architect great enough in
brain to throw a dome over the vast room
of St. Peter's, other workmen should be glad
to gird themselves for the task of putting
down some marble floors under the dome and
for the task of fastening some marble saints
to the walls.

But to recall to-day the many sides of this
personal force and beauty would consume
many an hour. His death does not sadden
us by only its own single, dark shadow, but
also by its reminder that a great troop of these
mighty ones is marching down into death's
valley. Mr. Beecher's death seems the death
of a generation. The Parkers, the Phillipses,
the Sumners, the Chases, the Lincolns, the
Grants—freedom's thinkers, freedom's orators, freedom's poets, freedom's statesmen,
freedom's soldiers—are hurrying away from
our world, and are leaving to new hands
interests the greatest ever committed to
mind and heart. There must be a great
Fatherland to which these citizens repair

because they have accomplished their tasks in the world. We can survive their loss if the new multitude will read their lives, mark their motives of action, their high politics, their simple but divine religion, and if their tombs shall become places where youth shall bow in tears and deep thoughtfulness, and as at the altars of God make solemn vows of lifelong service to mankind.

VII

PHILLIPS BROOKS[1]

IT would be an act of ingratitude were this country to pass in silence the death of Phillips Brooks. All our churches lay within borders of his bishopric. When, two or three years ago, in a loftiness of body which was only an emblem of a loftiness of mind, this preacher walked down this aisle to join you in worship, you all felt as though he were an elder brother in your religious family, and had come to visit his kin. Many of you, when spending a Sunday in the city where this modern apostle spoke, went joyfully to hear words which you knew would fall like manna from the sky. At last each of you seemed to hold some personal interest in Phillips Brooks; and now to-day we must all come up to his memory bringing our tears. Chosen Bishop of Massachusetts in 1891, the new title could not make much headway against the name of Phillips. In

[1] Died January 23, 1893.

instances not a few, when the title of "Bishop" is conferred upon a preacher, it does not take the previous name of the man more than a few minutes to get out of the way. If large bodies move slowly, the converse ought to be true and tell us why, often, when a common preacher is made Bishop, his name as a human being instantly disappears. In the case of this great friend who has bidden us "good-bye," the human being could not be easily displaced by any office in the gift of the church. As the names of Edmund Burke and William Pitt and Daniel Webster never needed any decoration from the catalogue of epithets, thus the name of Phillips Brooks did not take kindly to any form of prefix or supplement. If the peculiar duties of the office could have gone without carrying a title with them, the scene would have been happier; but to attempt to confer upon Phillips Brooks a title was too much like painting the pyramids.

William Pitt was called the "Great Commoner," not only because he was a member of the "House," but because he was by nature a dealer in the most universal of ideas—those ideas which were good not only for royal families but for all mankind. When

the Colonies attempted to secure their right
from the Crown, Mr. Pitt gave his eloquence to the cause of the Colonies, because
his mind could see the human race more
easily than it could see the little group of
grandees with the King at their head. Into
the mind of Pitt all the human rights which
had been detected and expressed between the
Greek period and the time of the Earl of
Chatham crowded to be reloved and re-
spoken. As science deals in the universal
truth about trees or stones or stars, so
William Pitt dealt in the propositions which
held true in all lands.

In the vast empire of religions Phillips Brooks was the "Great Commoner."
Whether his mind passed through the pages
of the Gospel, or read as best it could the
history of the primitive church, or read the
confessions of Augustine and saw him pick
up a psalter or heard him pray for the dead,
or if he read all over the dogmas and practices of the Roman Catholic fathers, he always emerged from the study infatuated
with only those truths and customs which
seemed most needful to the character and
salvation of the human multitude. He never
possessed the power to turn a little incident

into a great doctrine. He could not by any
means mistake a piece of the cross for a
potency which could heal disease ; nor was he
able to look upon a lighted candle as playing
any part in any form of natural or revealed
religion. He stood at that point where all
the Christian sects meet. No preacher could
go to Christ without seeing this brother as
being in the same path. All denominations
walked with him and enjoyed a conversation
which made their hearts burn on the way.
He was like that lofty arch in Paris towards
which all the great streets seem to run.
When we think of the discords which are
now sounding all through the field of both
the Catholic and Protestant denominations,
we must recall Phillips Brooks as the recon-
ciliation of the Nineteenth Century.

But no one who loves war can fill the
office of such a "great commoner." That
fame must rest on an intellect which is
wreathed with the garlands of peace. This
man did not fight the Ritualists or the
Romanists ; he came forward with the large
and positive truths of religion and permitted
all that was false or little to die of neglect.
His pulpit was so full of light that his people
forgot to bring candles to the chancel ; the

fragrance of the Gospel was so exceeding sweet that no acolytes were needed to swing smoking censers in front of the holy altar. We, too, have sat before him when the light was all in his forehead and the incense all in his heart.

In the late generations the Episcopal Church has been producing some great men. When the clergy of that denomination in England had become remarkable for the absence of learning and piety, and remarkable for the presence of ignorance, indolence and vice; when few who wore the name of clergyman possessed education enough to compose a sermon, and had not piety enough to care for the parish whose taxes they consumed, the Wesleyan reform sprang up. That effort was wholly a contempt for a dead sanctuary and an ardent longing for a religion like that of the Saviour of men. It was a new effort to rescue the tomb of Christ from the hand of the new infidels.

Jonathan Swift and Laurence Sterne had divided their time between the writings for the pulpit and writings for the promotion of depravity. Sterne published a few sermons, but his literary books were so disreputable that the sermons were soon forgotten in the pleasure which the vulgarity of "Tristram Shandy" gave to that age. It was the prevalence of such churchmen that compelled Wesley to rise up in behalf of a Christian life that bade fair to be forgotten. Wesleyism did not contemplate a new church; it was an uprising against ecclesiastical infamy. Awakened by Wesleyism, the National Episcopacy underwent a great reform and ran boldly forward.

A pulpit paid by national taxes easily falls from virtue, and, as often there were parochial schools where the teacher regularly drew a salary from the state but had an empty schoolhouse, so there were pulpits which gave a living to some man in holy orders, who seldom read a service and still less frequently wearied himself or an audience with a discourse. It is now about fifty years since there came to the English Episcopal Church a second great impulse. It was not wholly a reform, but it poured into that old sanctuary so much new piety and enthusiasm that it cannot but be called a marked part of a forward movement. It passes now in history under any one of several names: the "tractarian movement," or the "high-church movement," or the

" ritualistic movement," or " Puseyism." A few minds, deeply religious,—men who in the Seventeenth Century would have been the companions of Fénelon—began to study the far-off church of the fathers. They longed to rebuild their plundered and razed Jerusalem. In the long reign of vice and neglect even the beautiful buildings of God had become battered ruins. The house was as fallen as the heart.

These men, sons of Oxford, went back in history to find that day of splendour at which the worship of God began to sink. They shovelled away the earth from their buried Pompeii and soon found the rich old colours upon the long-hidden walls. It was a most valuable labour of history and love, for out of it came the rebuilding and repairing of the churches and chapels of England; and came also a living religion which joined a pure belief to a holy life. Hundreds of millions of dollars soon went into the rebuilding of the houses of religion; but there is no money which can express the new Christianity which began at once to re-adorn the soul.

The men who came back from that historic study, and who joined in this pious renaissance, soon divided into two classes, the High church and Low church, the former comprising those men who brought back all the rites and emblazonry of the earlier times, while the Low church became eclectic, and, feeling that the present had outgrown the emblematic period, asked England to accept the simple religion of Jesus and His apostles. The High church became enamoured of all they discovered and made valuable old attitudes, old positions, a facing the east, showy vestments, priestly offices, candles, incense, confessional, and many a genuflection.

These were the Ritualists, with whom the sandal of a Christ was the essential part of the Saviour of mankind. The Low church became equally enamoured only of that part of the New Testament which they found in the old lava beds, and, making of little moment the robes and motions and incense of the remote yesterday, they espoused a Christianity which reached out a kind hand towards the sects which had filed down from Calvin and Wesley. The High church used its relics for building a wall around itself. And thus it stands to-day, walled in, and as exclusive as though it feared that its friendship might escape and be wasted upon a Presbyterian

or a Wesleyan, and as though the love of
God might escape and invade some meeting-
house which did not make the sign of the
cross, or might escape and save some infant
that was dying at midnight without being
baptized.

It cannot in reason be charged upon the
Ritualists that they make religion too ornate.
Man has not lived in this world long enough
to enable him to say that any part of life can
hold too much of real beauty. The temperate
zone from the Gulf to the St. Lawrence is
beautiful in June, but it has never dared
laugh at the more abundant blossomings of
the tropics. Many of us have had happy
moments in those sanctuaries where grand
choral music has marched up and down and
in and out.

There may be other minds which love to
face the east, and other minds which love to
see incense rising as though it were carrying
heavenward the burden of human prayers.
Persons of little or much culture must be
eclectics in the realm of beauty for the
church, or the city, or the home. If the
ritualists feel proud of a pictured religion,
and ask that many texts of Scripture be uttered in material emblems, and that the

candles of Solomon's Temple reappear in the modern house of God, they have a taste we are all bound to respect. We concede the same right to those Christians who love the rite of washing each other's feet. We confess sympathy with the ritualism of the Salvation Army, which pictures Christ as the Captain of their host and which follows Paul in the dream of being a good soldier of the Lord. Let ritualism appear where it may, in the High church, or the Roman church, or in the Salvation Army, it must pass along as a lawful form and variation of human taste. Its harmfulness has of late years come from minds, which, instead of admiring and enjoying Ritualism, have descended to the worship of it—the worship of such fugitive and unimportant accessories—which made it difficult for a Bishop's crown to reach a forehead which loved the sublime spirituality of Jesus more than it loved the fleeting pageantry of perfumes and colours, and which loved the face turned towards all the sects in their hour of prayer more than he loved a genuflection or a face turned towards the east.

In the east we see only the sun, but all around this man lay the hopes and griefs of

the human soul, more tremendous than a
thousand suns. If any proof were wanting,
to show that Ritualism, when idolized, turns
men who might have been scholars and
thinkers and orators into half-childish
natures, busy in the ornaments of an altar,
like children around the Christmas tree, that
proof may be read in the difficulties which
lay between Phillips Brooks and the high
office for which he seemed to have been
born. In itself, Ritualism may be a lawful
form of religion, but history shows that it
may be cultivated until it excludes what it
once ornamented, and ends by becoming
only the tropical efflorescence of human
vanity. A deep attachment to Ritualism
may be taken as a good-bye bidden by the
young preacher to the height and depth of
thought which belongs to the pulpit in all
the great period of church life. A high
Ritualism is a most perfect and most alluring
means for keeping the mind of the clergyman
within the limits of a perpetual childhood.
A Ritualist ought to admire his ceremony as
a man loves flowers—happy when the blossoms are near, but happy also in the barren
fields of winter or in Sahara's leafless sand.

If one thinks of the High churchmen and

the Low churchmen as visiting the old past
to find once again the lost church of the
fathers, one must see the Ritualist entering
our age, not only bringing much of the
apostolic doctrine, but also as having his
arms full of candles, of priestly robes, of
curtains fastened by "loops of blue each to
its sister," and full of "badger-skins dyed
red"; and the same spectator must see the
Low churchman coming from that act of exhuming, carrying in his hands the words and
deeds and life of our Lord. You may all, if
you wish, admire many a High churchman
acting in his peculiar office, but for this
absent Bishop you cannot but cherish a
greater admiration and a deeper love. He
reached out his hand to all men, and so sin-
cere was he that his hand always pointed out
the path of his heart.

When the heart studies the bygone years,
it ought to esteem great in the past that
which it wishes to come true in the future.
We ought to look deeply at the yesterdays
in order to catch the image of to-morrow.
And, as the soul of Phillips Brooks longed to
see a Christian unity and equality, longed to
see a civilization which should resemble the
life of the Son of Man, he gathered up from

the fathers the doctrines which tended to make noble men and to join them into a wide brotherhood. The Ritualists seem, by some error of locality, to have exhumed the Mosaic age; the Low churchmen seem to have laid open to view a more recent arena —that of Jesus.

In his wanderings in the old religious world, this lamented mortal recalls that Dante who, in his great dream, drew near a holy mountain, which lifted up its form not far from the Paradise of his God. The devout wanderer did not see any candles or vestments or studied posturing; he saw no "apostolic succession." The world around him was too great to be in harmony with the rites and emblems of some fleeting year. One by one the angels came over him, but each one was chanting some benediction which had once fallen from the lips of the Master. No sooner had the words sounded, "Blessed are the pure in heart," than on came some other winged choristers saying, "Blessed are the merciful." To the same Italian worshipper at last a great chorus chanted the Lord's Prayer, all amplified like a tune in music which breaks up into four parts:

The Message of David Swing

"Oh, Thou Almighty Father! Who dost make
The heavens Thy dwelling, not in bounds confined,
But that with love intenser there Thou viewest
Thy primal effluence, hallowed be Thy name!
Join each created being to extol
Thy might, for worthy humblest thanks and praise
Is Thy blessed Spirit. May the Kingdom's peace
Come unto us, for we, unless it come,
With all our striving thither tend in vain."

These are the words which our great
American "Commoner" heard chanted in
the lofty cathedrals of the past, and these
are the words he wished to hear sounding in
the greater aisles and corridors of the future.
He extracted greatness from the past because
he wished history to be only another name
for his soul's hope. His mind conceived of a
service and an anthem too great to be read
or sung by his limited sect. His ritual must
include a hundred Books of Common Prayer;
his vestments must include the robes of a
Louis XIV, the habit of an exiled Quaker,
and the seamless coat of Jesus. He found
his universal and perpetual harmony in the
words: "Blessed are the pure in heart."

If you would find a reason for the confessed eloquence of this eminent Christian,
you must begin by studying the advantage
found in a mind which loved the whole hu-

152

man family, and then loved all the great
truths which hold the people's happiness.
Eloquence is the utterance of great truths in
a manner worthy of the truths. But there
can be no such utterance without passion.
This man was capable of loving even the
negro slave. When those old days of trial
were brooding over the Nation, Phillips
Brooks flamed up on the slaves' side. After
the slaves were free he travelled a thousand
miles to plead in this city for the cause of
the education and full citizenship of those
homeless Africans. Only a little group of
our citizens appeared in the large hall, for
the orator was young in his fame and the
city was young in its power to appreciate
such an appeal from heart to heart. None
the less did the speech run like molten iron
from a furnace, thus teaching us who listened
that oratory is great truth uttered with great
passion. Gesture and tone are insignificant.

It is necessary for this truth and passion
to enjoy the noble accessories of language
and style. It is difficult for a great mind,
great heart, great language, and good style,
all to meet in one human being. The dis-
tance between orators is therefore very great.
Only a few come to us each hundred years.

In Bishop Brooks, all these ingredients mingled. He had by nature and by study mastered the one language of his race. It became at last the hundred gates of his soul's Thebes. At these portals the riches of his age passed in and out. He used no dead words, no old, worn-out phrases, at which the brain of the listener sinks to sleep. His words were all alive, and they came singing like the string and arrows of the wonderful bow of Ulysses. His words came too rapidly indeed, but his ideas were instantly seen and instantly felt to be true. Each word was distinct, like a single note in some rapid melody, an inseparable part of a beautiful song.

What a simplicity there is in all such high speech! because the theme is so large and so absorbing that it shames away the most of artifice, and makes the little art of the piece wholly invisible. If those final words ascribed to the Bishop were indeed spoken, his mind was not greatly under a cloud, for the simple sentence whispered to a servant: "You need not care for me longer; I am going home," is made of the kind of words which earth needs when it is fading, and which the final home asks for when it is

opening its gates to a noble spirit, once a
pilgrim here. Death always asks for simple
language, because its mystery and sadness
and hope are all the ornamentation the
speaker or listener can bear. Ah! sad loss
such a being to all the churches of our country! He was a man so symmetrical and so
fitted to all the hours and need of our land
that the office of bishop went to him, not to
add anything to his fame or power, but to
be itself honoured and exalted. It was the
office that went to be crowned. As an Episcopal bishop he was much less than as the
great, free orator of the Christian philosophy.
But the terms "bishop" and "commoner"
are both made sacred now by the sudden ad-
vent of death.

It is certain that this name will long remain the centre of a magic power. The
Baptist, with his close communion, cannot
but be impressed with that scene of brotherhood which lies so outspread in this churchman's life; the Unitarians can also look
towards Phillips Brooks, to know how
rationalism of a high school may be joined
to the most marked spirituality and piety;
the restless and debating Presbyterians may
study him, to learn what peace and useful-

ness they can find in a Christianity many
times simpler than their Confession of Faith;
to him may the Low church look for perpetual vindication; and to him should all the
young ritualistic clergy turn, not to abandon
their pictured and highly coloured worships,
but to mark how the pulpit of a Christian
teacher and thinker towers above the swing-
ing of censers and the adjustment of robes
and the graceful bowing of the body in its
acts of devotion. He should warn them
against the folly of a half-wasted life.

While we are thus standing by such a
grave, the inquiry comes from many whether
Ritualism and Romanism are to displace the
simpler churches and come into almost
despotic power. Of this result there seems
little probability. The Broad church is
young, but Ritualism is as old as the world.
It ruled in the Mosaic age. It ruled in
India, Egypt, and in all great nations before
the Son of Man came, and then entering
Christianity it filled with its pageant all
temples up to the days of Luther.

The Broad church has been in the world
only half a century. In that brief period
what master minds it has produced! It is
nothing else than the old Christianity of

rites and doctrines smitten by the deeper thought of these later generations. That reason which has created the modern world will most surely drive religion towards a holy life, a simple piety and a wide brotherhood. Romanism will be smitten by the same hand, and one by one shall fall from it the follies and vices which that Church gathered up by passing through the middle centuries of ignorance and sin. That new thought, which has transformed despotisms into republics and slaves into the citizens of England and France, will not spare the old life and ideas of the temple of prayer. The antiquity of Romanism and Ritualism will not protect them. Many things thousands of years old have died in this century. It is the great graveyard of antiquity and the beautifully draped cradle of a new youth.

When it is said that reason will smite the old churches, it is not meant that any violence will come. Heaven keep violence far away from all those Roman and Protestant altars where our parents said their prayers! Reason will smite them only as it smote the valley of the Mississippi and covered it with civilization; smite them only as the sun smites the fields in April and makes them bloom;

smite them as reason touched Phillips Brooks
when he was young and made his heart
warm with love and his forehead white with
pure truth.

VIII

DECORATION DAY

TO-MORROW the graves of the soldiers are to be decorated by the hands of memory and esteem. Many thousand persons will pay thus the tribute of personal love. Many a mother will visit the spot where her son sleeps; many a man and a woman, now in middle life, will visit the grave where their father rests. He marched to war when they were little children. They remember some noise of drums and some sad parting; they remember the body came back and that the neighbours met to hold a funeral service. To-morrow old letters will be re-read and old photographs restudied with many a tear.

A few days before the battle of Stone River a young husband, a colonel of cavalry, left Cincinnati in haste, to resume his place with his troopers. He foresaw a great battle. He wrote a good-bye note to his wife, saying that 'a great battle was near; he might fall;

she must not wear mourning; she must plant
some vines by his grave, and go on as though
in the world of a great and kind God.' In
a few days that awful meeting of armies
came, and this colonel was among the slain.
Thus tens of thousands of graves will to-
morrow be visited by hearts full of an affection which no years can abate. Many will
say: Here my father sleeps; here my brother,
here my cousin, here my classmate, turns to
dust. But as that generation of weepers
will soon all be silent as the soldiers, will
soon overtake them in the great halting-
place, this Decoration Day will soon rest upon
the gratitude which a Nation owes to its defenders and upon the admiration all noble
minds cherish for men who were heroic
enough to imperil their life for their country.
Each soldier's monument in the cities and
cemeteries of the land will be decorated to-
morrow; not in the name of personal friendship only, but also in the name of that intelligence and self-denial which could fight and
die for the welfare of society. Even when
the public shall not know even the names of
the entombed soldiers it will cast down its
offerings to their virtues.

It adds much to the beauty of to-morrow

that all the wars of our Nation have been honourable. Exception must be made in the case of the war with Mexico in 1846. That conflict with a neighbour was brought about by the Southern clamour for more slave territory. Texas must be annexed with or without the consent of Mexico. The Union would at once be dissolved unless the South were granted this new era. With a view to such annexation, Mr. Polk, of Tennessee, was elected President and soon came annexation and war. The other struggles—that of 1776, of 1812 and of 1861—were founded upon great principles of right, and they stand in history all ennobled by the calmest thought, truth and honour. Out of these three struggles our Nation extracted those principles and that power which make it at last such a home for so many millions. Whoever will to-day make a survey of this Nation and mark the blessings and opportunities it confers upon its citizens will not fail to whisper his gratitude to all those men who gave up their lives in those fields of battle.

Those dark days which came between 1860 and 1865 were gloomy beyond the realization of any of those who were then

children. The loyal States were full of all
the sorrows which wars entail. Values were
all unsettled, literature, education, and all
art had come to a halt. The heart was full
of depression lest England might join in the
Confederacy.

Defeats, carnage, blunders, great expense,
new calls for troops, mourning in all cities
and villages found a procession of ideas as
gloomy as the ideal march of death. Thousands of the noblest men in the North were
so depressed by the awful surroundings that
they said to each other in private: " Perhaps
it would have been better to let the slave
States withdraw in peace." The outcome of
war was as much hidden in 1862 as it was in
1776. However patriotic and brave a man
may be, his heart can easily become the
victim of doubts. It is easy now for our
young generation to look back upon the last
war and see it as only a long march of an
invincible army. An army led by men who
did not know defeat and who had little to
do except shout victory behind a running
enemy. So Franklin in later life could look
back with pleasure to the time when he was
poor and homeless, but it was not in his
power when he had only the loaf of bread to

look forward with much of romantic poetry.
Thus our new millions can look back upon
the war of the Union and see a fine procession
of statesmen marching towards universal
liberty, but those who marched and those
who led thirty years ago could not gaze upon
any such a scene, there being a thick, black
curtain between them and the future.

There was in the North and in Canada a
party formed in the name of a disgraceful
peace. They talked of conventions of the
Middle States; talked of a new separate West,
and never used any language about the
Union except that of despair. These men
once sent word from Canada to Mr. Lincoln
that they were empowered to negotiate a
peace. Patriots feared that there would be a
guerilla conflict for twenty years. The sud-
denness with which the war at last ended, the
sudden acceptance of the defeat by the entire
South came to the whole world as a great
surprise. The soldiers whose names we are
to honour not only fought for their country,
but they fought, suffered, and died amid
great gloom. They could not see a final
perfect triumph—they could only toil and
hope. To suffer, to be wounded, to die on
the eve of an assured victory might be a

form of blessedness; but heavy were the hearts which had to endure agony without being able to read the future of the contest.

A Greek orator who had to speak at Athens after a very disastrous battle said that the true soldier never dies defeated, for, go as the battle may, there is victory always in his soul. It must have been thus with the defenders of our Union. They must have been so full of the sense of right and duty that in prison or in the hospital or dying on the field, their minds must have been filled with triumph. In one of the darkest hours of the whole strife those disunionists who had assembled in Canada asked permission to come to Washington and submit to the President some terms of peace. Mr. Lincoln sent word that he would give them an audience only in case their plans involved the restoration of the Union and the abolition of slavery; there could be no peace on any other terms. Thus with Mr. Lincoln, however dark the battle-field, there was always a victory in his heart.

It must have been thus with the rank and file in their last hour. Sinking away upon the bloody field, while their eyes were taking a last look at the picture of wife and child or father or mother, those noble men must have felt within the triumph of the most divine right. The cause was one of the greatest for which arms ever clashed.

The Greeks and Romans often made war only through vanity, or else that they might plunder a rich neighbour. Napoleon marched 600,000 men against Moscow only because the Czar of Russia would not close the Russian harbour to English ships. Here in America the contest was for the preservation of the best nation ever founded in the whole history of man, a nation whose principles had been selected from the wisdom of all ages and which had been made into a State by the wisest and best of all men, principles which for nearly a hundred years had brought to millions of citizens the most possible of prosperity and happiness.

But this Nation so famous for its men and ideas contained one dark spot. It contained a blemish which France, Germany, England and Russia would not permit to soil their fame. At last the hour came in which the question must be settled whether the blemish must be continued and the Nation destroyed, or whether the Nation should be preserved and the spot erased. Thus came a war not of vanity or conquest, but a struggle to save the wisdom of ages. By a singular mental misfortune there was a group of Confederate citizens who loved slavery more than they loved freedom; they had reached the singular wisdom which could love the spots on the sun more than they loved the sun, loved the worm in a rose more than they loved the rose itself.

When it is remembered that under the war lay such a noble groundwork of right and truth it ought not to be difficult for us to feel that our Nation's dead died in peace, even on the fields of defeat; it ought not to be difficult for us to cast flowers upon their tombs. We ought to feel that no soul can be prolific enough in blossoms to equal the moral excellence of the day.

All the happiness, all the success, all the splendour of the present combine to enhance the honour of the soldier's grave. The mind can easily make here and now a picture of certain beautiful forms going forth to-morrow to honour the patriotic dead. The form of Religion happy in her new truth and new morality; the form of Politics, set free from an old wrong; Education widened and enriched; Art quickened and exalted; Literature newly inspired ; the South awakened to personal industry and full of new dreams ; the South and North holding hands in friendship :—these graceful figures can be seen as hovering like blest angels over the soldiers' dust and saying in simple gratitude, " Soldier of the Nation, we thank thee with full heart."

All the prosperous cities and towns which are now redeeming the South, the growing unity of language, literature, social life and political doctrine and sentiment, come to us from those battle-fields whose memory returns in each May. It would have been more in harmony with all religion and all philosophy could the establishment of the Union and the abolition of slavery have come by peaceful ways and means, but since this was impossible, unable now to amend the past, we must go back to all those bloody grounds and bless them that, out of such sufferings, they grew for an age so many flowers. In the name of a noble Nation, all united from Gulf to Lake and from sea to sea, in the name of the advance of all that is good, in the name of inventions, discoveries, sciences, arts, a happier womanhood, a happier childhood, a nobler manhood, we this

day declare fragrant and precious all those
flowers which send their roots down into our
soldiers' dust. The events which have followed the dreadful war have justified its
years of deep sorrow. The bitterness has
all passed, the days of peace have come.

No one who attempts to-day to speak in
the name of both religion and the soldier
will dare pass by the fact that the African,
although free from the chains of a slave, is
still the victim of a wide-spread injustice.
He is still too often treated as an animal not
worthy of human rights. Against the con-
tinuance of the old slave-driving theory, all
honourable men, white and black, must
think and act ; but at the same time our coloured citizens must give the South credit for
having made a very great progress in its
opinions and conduct. A new era is coming,
but all men must lament that it comes in
slowly.

Our public men are simply the creatures
of the age. Our Presidents move very
slowly for fear they may walk away from
that ballot-box which is to contain the war-
rant of a second term. Our only hope lies
in such an awakening of the people as shall
at last make justice to the African citizen a

matter of life and death to the men who want high office. We must make opinions for years and years before we can make great statesmen.

The "second term" must be abolished, and then must come one more reform, that of making to a common, scheming, soulless politician even a first term impossible. A President of such a Nation ought not to be a tame follower of old, beaten political paths. He ought to be a humane man, a lover of even the poor; capable like Christ of blessing the multitude with new beatitudes straight from heaven. Since Mr. Lincoln there has been no president who revealed any marked humane sentiments. Exception may well be made in the person of President Hayes. He did what he could for the freedom of the South. He would have done more had not his term been full of the troubles which were yet strong and fresh from the war of the rebellion. But with Mr. Hayes humanity disappeared. However great in many particulars the Presidents may have been, no one of them has been visibly affected by the fact that the negro in the South cannot vote in safety and is liable any day to be imprisoned, whipped, hanged, or

burned. Had Henry Bergh been President
in any one of the late Presidential periods,
he would have found some means of check-
ing that cruelty which so shames our civilization. But literature, the daily press, the
pulpit, all good men and women, North and
South, will have to be active some years yet
before a refined civilization, one of love and
justice, will be able to trample to dust that
stereotyped soul, the calculating political
character, which is so utterly and forever
heartless.

The same slow progress which gave the
African liberty must go onward and clothe
him with every form of human right. The
soldiers whose graves are so sacred must be
ornamented not only by floral offerings but
also by the ever-growing happiness of the
whole people. Our troops did not fight and
die for these May lilies, roses and laurels,
but they did for humanity, and their most
worthy Decoration Day will come in only
that spring which shall say to their disem-
bodied souls: "Every human being in the
Union is living in the fullness of confessed
and secured right."

Towards such a noble result we must all
struggle with daily industry and with daily

hope. As the churches are now attempting
to get Calvinism out of their creeds, and are
no longer willing to disgrace the Deity by
making Him select a few men for happiness
and doom others to wrath, so must we elimi-
nate such a philosophy from the Nation and
save it from the disgrace of electing white
men to mercy and dooming black men to the
jail and rope and malicious fire. Let not
those at least rail at Calvinism who conduct
a Nation in the name of a most infamous
reprobation.

The right has this fact to encourage it—
that the American public has always sooner
or later made its moral force felt in law and
conduct. Its words of truth and pleadings
have never been lost. The daily press, the
magazines and reviews, the graver literature,
the schoolhouse, the pulpit, have always
compelled the darkness to flee and light to
come. These voices can once more penetrate
the clouds and usher in a happier day to
souls that have been wronged for three hundred years. If not many years ago there
was a vast multitude of persons who died on
bloody fields for human rights and happiness,
is there not now living a still more numerous
army who will live in flowery states, in a

blossoming world, for an advance of the same right and happiness? Will you not all live for principles for which your brothers died? The South is herself beginning to speak and act in behalf of the rights of the African. Such wise words and deeds are worthy of being reprinted all through the land and of being expanded into full eloquence.

Let us pass from this plea for the African and take one more view of the soldier's grave. Each year lessens the discord between the North and South and increases the harmony. What our country now needs is not a host of recriminating historians, but a host of brotherly souls bound up in a new future. Never was adequate justice done the judgment and feelings of Charles Sumner when, soon after the close of the rebellion, he moved in the Senate that "no name of any battle-field of the war be placed upon the Nation's flag and that the Capitol should contain on its walls no picture of a battle in which citizens fought citizens." The motion was ridiculed by many Northern Senators and editors of that day, but the lapse of years has shown the idea just and beautiful. No American ever surpassed Charles Sumner in the conception and defense of human rights, but he was incapable of worshipping war between brothers. He gladly washed all such battle pictures from his remembrance. His spirit ought to become rapidly the spirit of our Nation in its entire extent. Hate must be transient, love eternal.

That breadth of mind and soul which made Charles Sumner so impressive is moving over the South and is liable to adorn that warm heart whose love and philosophy were repressed by the presence and use of human bondage. There remains nothing to prevent a oneness of idea from prevailing between Chicago and Memphis and Atlanta.

A Confederate officer in an essay contributed recently to a literary magazine of Dallas, Texas, having summed up his sad memories of the war, adds these words: "Peace and happiness reign supreme over a free people. Our hearts are great enough to love our whole country, North and South, mountain, river and plain. The gulf breezes waft soft messages from orange bowers to Northern hills and apple blossoms. . . . We are all Americans. We are all patriots. Thus let it be forever." Thus this brilliant essay of J. R. Cole reveals the fact that the graves of the soldiers imply a national unity of principles and a wide-spread oneness of heart. Many years ago the words "impending crisis" and "irrepressible conflict" were upon the lips of all statesmen. How could slavery and liberty dwell in the same house? All we need know to-day is that the land is full of soldiers' graves and those words are gone. There is no "impending crisis," the "irrepressible conflict" has passed away. The blood of our brothers has purchased the unity and happiness of a great people. One justice, one truth, one duty, one hope, are slowly advancing as though like morning sunbeams they were anxious to flood all fields with one light.

When to-morrow you shall look at monuments and graves of the known and the nameless dead, tears ought to fill your eyes at the thought of the thirty years in which those hearts have been absent from the scenery and experience of this life. On your account they are absent from your world. But such tears meet the demand which the soldier's tomb makes upon the soul of every living citizen. When Pericles attempted to comfort the Athenians at the graves of their soldiers he told them that at best 'earth was the sepulchre of a vast multitude of illustrious men. It was only a large grave.' But this is the comfort of an iron-like fate. It is not adequate to our greater age. We need a richer philosophy. We must say that through these scattered hillocks, with their May ornaments of grass and garlands, there comes to us the voice of God and man, earth and sky saying, Catch from these braves their spirit; take up the banners of truth their dying hands let fall; as they made a greater nation, so go ye on to make the grander Republic a greater art, a greater learning, a greater justice, a greater friendship, a greater religion. The souls of the soldiers are not in these graves. They are far away on diviner heights. So those who to-morrow shall strew lilies must at once turn away from those heaps of dust and look up towards nobler heights in religion and in all the blessed forms of love and righteousness. Such death must be the inspiration of life.

IX

THE DUTY OF THE PULPIT

In the Hour of Social Unrest

IT would be a happiness to all of us, could we meet to-day having in our hands branches from the woods or shells from the shore where we may have recently attempted to find pleasure and rest: but the events of the last few months, and the gloom of the future, have stolen from prairie and seacoast their long-found charm.

The trees and the waters have for many weeks past sighed over the infirmities of our country.

To find the images of greatness, we have been compelled to look into the past. When President Cleveland intervened, and, perhaps, saved this city from being plundered and burned, some men feared to thank him for such a quick intervention. July must deal very gently with criminals who are to vote in November.

Not since 1861 has the sky been as dark as it is to-day.[1] We have unconsciously built up within this generation two black passions —the one, the feeling that money is the only thing worth living for, and the other, that work must hate capital. Thus the level of all society is lowered—the moneyed class by its worship of gold, the other class by its life of hate. While wealth has inflamed its possessors and worshippers, there has lived and talked an army of angry orators, whose purpose has been to make the men who work in the vineyard hate the men who pay them at nightfall. In such circumstances, the vineyard will soon be, first, a battle-field, and then, a desert.

It would seem that all the Christian clergy, Catholic and Protestant, and all the ethical teachers should, this autumn, enter into a new friendship with these two discordant classes, and preach to both alike the gospel of a high humanity. The churches and pulpits of all grades possess a vast influence. They do not hold any "key to the situation," or any "balance of power"; they cannot open and close the gates of the earthly heaven and hell for America; but they

[1] September, 1894.

possess an enormous moral force—a power that should no longer be exhausted upon little theological issues and practices. All the intellectual and spiritual resources of the pulpit should be exhausted in the effort to advance human character. Society needs speedy and large additions to both its righteousness and its common sense.

What saved the country from a great calamity last July was the fact that the schoolhouse, the church, and the press, of the last fifty years had quietly created an intelligence large enough to stand between the people and their ruin. When the new kind of autocrat ordered all the railway wheels between the two oceans to stop, and had sat down to enjoy the silence of locomotives and iron rails, there were so many noble and educated men in the railway service that the voice of the autocrat was the only noise that died out. It was not President Cleveland alone that came between us and a great calamity. He was aided by the high common sense of a large majority of the railway employees. The railway union of working men was not formed for a career of mingled cruelty and nonsense, but that men might help each other in honourable ways and in hours of great wrong and need. The union was not formed in order that railway men might become beggars, at a time when their work was bringing almost a barrel of flour a day for each family. With wages at two dollars a day and wheat at half a dollar a bushel, the strike and trouble of July were not only unreasonable but malicious.

Nearly all clergymen stand close to the people. They are reared in the philosophy that gives bread to the hungry. The gospel of Christ is one of infinite sympathy. Men who from choice enter the ministry of the Judæan religion are never so happy as when they see the labourer sit down under a good roof to a table spread with abundant food. In the life of the average clergyman, a large part of his thought and public utterance, and actual labour and sympathy, is given to what is called the common people. The upper classes need little. There is nothing in the millionaire that appeals to the heart. The rich are so self-adequate that they may draw admiration and esteem, but not sympathy. The heart of the pulpit is freely given to the middle and lower classes. In all time, the common people have attracted

to themselves the most of both philosophy
and poetry, but the attention and the affection they won in the former times seem
weak, compared with the love that has been
flung to them in the passing century. Under
the influence of this sympathetic philosophy,
wages have been advanced, humane laws
have been passed, the facts of health and
disease have been studied, and new action
has come with new light; and when into
such an age of both inquiry and action there
is projected such a scene as that of last July,
the spectacle does not belong to reason or
humanity, but only to despotic ignorance and
ill will.

Labour may, and even must, organize; but
the labourers must organize as just and law-
abiding men, country-loving men, and not as
bandits. The depressing memory of last
July is not to be found in the fact that
labour was organized, or wholly in the fact
that it "struck." The strike was, indeed, perfectly destitute of common sense, but the
chief disgrace of the hour lay in the willing-
ness of free men to obey a central despot and
join in such acts of wrong and violence as
would have disgraced savages. Benevolence
is humiliated that it must feed and clothe

men who will break the skull or kick to
insensibility the brother who wishes to earn
bread for his hungry family.

It was discovered last July that some of
the labour unions employ fighting men to go
to and fro to hunt up and knock down those
who do not join in the folly—those who are
satisfied with their wages or who must work.
Not every workman is a trained pugilist.
So men are hired to spend the day or the
week in pounding men who are noble and
industrious. The cry "I am an American"
does not avail as much in Chicago as the
words "I am a Roman" availed Paul in
Jerusalem. When Paul said he was a Roman,
the mob fell back; but when Mr. Cleveland
said, "These pounded men are Americans,"
it was thought by some that he was not the
proper person to make the remark. And yet
our pulpits have, for fifty years, been trying
to make Christians, and our schools and
printing-presses have been trying to endow
these Christians with sense.

Quite a number of clergymen have banded
together to preach the gospel of personal
righteousness; that Christianity is Christ in
human life, Christ in society, Christ in money,
and Christ in work. We preachers must all

come to that definition of the church. This
height of thought will make all dizzy for a
time; but the quality of our old Christianity
will not meet the demands of a republic. A
despotism may be sustained by Catholics or
Protestants, but a republic must be sustained
by men.

Labour guilds are as old as work and
capital; but one kind of labour guild is new,
and let us all pray that it shall not live to
become old. In the darkness of the Fourteenth Century, the young working man
looked happily forward to the day when
he could be admitted into the guild of his
craft. His mother and sisters looked after
his habits, that his character might be above
reproach. The approach to the initiation
day was much like a youth's approach to his
first communion. New clothes, a feast, new
conduct, new inspiration, new hopes came
with the hour that placed this new name
upon the noble roll. But this was in the
dark ages. In the close of the Nineteenth
Century, when the heavens and earth are
ablaze with the light of Christ, when love
for man is written everywhere in letters of
gold, when congresses of religion meet to
teach us that all men are brethren, then the

men who join a guild shake a bludgeon at
their brother and are advised by a reckless
king to buy a gun. Some men call this
phenomenon a commercial disturbance. It
is nothing of the kind. In the South Sea
Islands it is barbarism; among the carnivo-
rous animals it is called ferocity; in our
civilized land it is infamy.

It seems evident that Christianity asks
labourers to be organized into societies. If
a church may be organized that Christians
may help each other and confer with each
other about all things that pertain to the
church, why may not carpenters and railway
men form a union that many minds and
many hearts may find what is best for the
toilers in their field? The word "Church"
means a gathering of people, and if the
exigencies of religion may demand an assembly, so may the exigencies of a trade.
But none of these assemblages can sustain
any relations whatever to violence or any
kind of interference with the liberty or
rights of man. For a vast group of railway
men to sign away their personal liberty and
permit some one man to order them around
as though slaves, is a spectacle pitiful to look
upon; but to band together for interference

with the rights of man is, not a mental weakness, but a crime.

It is a great task for a labour guild to study and fully learn what are the facts and the needs of itself. Before men quit their employers, they should all know the reason of the move. After men have been idle for a winter and have come to regular work and regular pay, if they hasten to strike, their reason ought to be so large that the whole world can see it. But we do things differently in enlightened America. Our men hasten to throw down tools and their wages, and, at last, when starving, they ask some committee to make a microscopical search for the reason of the distress. And, before this reason is known, eminent men express themselves as in full sympathy with it. All the railway wheels in America were ordered to stop out of sympathy with a reason which a committee was looking for with a microscope. The railways were giving work to four millions of people. This work was all "called off" by a man with some telegraphic blanks, and the poor families supported by the Northwestern Railroad lost two hundred thousand dollars, the workmen of the Illinois Central one hundred and sixty-four thousand dollars, of the Milwaukee and St. Paul one hundred and seventy-five thousand dollars, and thus on to the millions—all which loss was ordered from sympathy with men who were getting each six hundred dollars a year.

Labour unions will waste their work by the millions of dollars' worth, and will soil their name and ruin the sympathy of literature, art and religion, as long as they trust their cause to hot-headed, ignorant, illogical men. Labour should have for its chieftains our Franklins or our John Stuart Mills. These should be its guide. If our land possesses no such minds, then are we on the eve of untold misfortune. When labour shall have Franklins for its walking delegates, it will enter upon a new career. Capital will confer with it, congresses of working men will meet, and men will find the wages of each toiler and of each new period; but nothing can be done by a foolish despot with a club. Yes, something can be done—the Republic can be hopelessly ruined through a ruined manhood.

The wages and whole welfare of the labouring man have been much advanced in twenty-five years, but the gun and club have taken no part in this progress. Conference, thought, reason, benevolence, have accom-

plished the blessed task, and they will do much
more when they are invited to help our race.
Moral power makes laws. It shames the
guilty. It dissolves adamant. It founded the
Christian Church. It has civilized whole
races; it has emancipated the mind; it has
freed slaves.

It may easily be remembered that a London
man a few years ago unveiled the wrongs
inflicted upon poor young girls. This injustice did not need to be examined by a
microscope. The heart of London became
aflame with indignation. The Archbishop
of Canterbury, and the Archbishop of West-
minster, Cardinal Manning, the Bishop of
London, Sir William Harcourt, and Sir
Robert Cross, flung their minds and hearts
into the cause, and the Parliament passed a
new law for a longer and diviner protection
of girls.

To many labour unions all talk of moral
power carries the weight of only nonsense.
The moral influence theory is indeed defective, but it is the only one within human
reach. If a dozen men should resolve that
they have rights to seats in a street car, their
theory seems good; but, on getting into one
of these vehicles, if they find the seats all

taken, unless they can club those persons out of those seats, the theory of those dozen unionists is very defective. When a man resolves that he ought to sit down and then stands up, his resolution is defective. But what makes it defective? The rights of the man who is sitting down. So when a set of men resolve that they will work only for four dollars a day, they hold an imperfect platform, because of the rights of the men who will work for three dollars. Should a clergyman resign his pulpit because his people will not pay him six thousand dollars a year, his theory is incomplete indeed, unless he can kill the preachers who will come for five thousand dollars. But he must go to and fro with his imperfect theory. It is spoiled by the rights of other preachers. Thus, against all labour unions not strictly moral, the laws of the human race rise up. The rights of mankind oppose them. All society is founded upon the rights of man—not of the man who works for three dollars a day, but of the man also who works for one dollar or for any sum whatever. Any force in a labour union means anarchy. A guild, without violence, may be imperfect, but, with violence, it is infamous.

Where would our city and perhaps our Nation have been in this September, had not the labourers in the town of Pullman and in the whole land been for the most part law-abiding? The churches may confess the rashness of the strike, but we must forgive the mistakes of those who respected the rights of mankind and the laws of the land. Many toilers were so patient and law-abiding as to give promise of being worthy citizens of a great country. What all those workmen need is a leadership worthy of their cause or their flag.

The flag of labour is a perfectly glorious one—too grand to be carried by a fanatic or a simpleton or a criminal. Capital is nothing until labour takes hold of it. A bag will hold money, but a bag cannot transform that money into an iron road, a bridge, a train of cars, an engine. An armful of bonds did not fling the bridge over the arm of the sea at Edinburgh; the bonds of England did not join the Mediterranean to the Red Sea; gold did not erect St. Peter's at Rome; nor did it lift up any of the sublime or beautiful things in any art. Money came along and attempted to buy the canvases of Angelo, but it did not paint them. The millions of people who came here last summer did not come to see the millions of money, but to see what labour had done with money, and they saw a great spectacle. What domes! What arches! What "Courts of Honour"! What canals! What statues! What machines! What pictures! What jewels! What thought! What taste! What love! And yet the whole scene was the matchless emblazonry of labour. As God manifests Himself in the external objects of earth and in the millions of stars, thus man speaks by his works, and in our world labour sits enthroned. Capital is a storehouse of seeds; labour is their field, their soil, their rain, and their summer time. Over a potency so vast and godlike, only Wisdom herself should preside. If our age has any great men—men whose hearts are warm and pure, and whose minds are large as the world,—it should ask them to preside over the tasks and wages of the labourer. Anarchy, Crime, and Folly should be asked to stand back. Those three demons may be called to the front when our labourers are seeking for poverty and disgrace.

You have all heard of the hostility of capital to labour. But there is no special truth in the phrase. Labour is just as hostile

to labour. The whole truth is this : Man is
not anxious to spend his money. There is a
saying that " the fool and his money are soon
parted," but we have not reached the maxim
that labour loves to make presents to labour.
Did you ever know a blacksmith who was
happy to pay large bills to the plumber ?
Are the carpenters anxious to have their
tailors advance the price of a suit of clothes ?
Are the " walking delegates " for the plaster-
ers anxious to pay the farmer a dollar for
wheat ? If reports be true, there are labouring men in the West who are so hostile to
the labour of their brothers that they are
going to buy most all needful things in the
shops of England.

Thus labour is as great an enemy of labour
as it is of capital. The hostility between
labour and money is a mischievous fiction,
gotten up by dreamers and professional
grumblers, who wish to ride into office or
fame by parading a love for the multitude.
This false love ought soon to end its destruc-
tive career. Last June and July it cost the
working men many millions of dollars. Had
some walking delegates of Christianity told
these men that labour and capital are eternal
friends —that labour is the language of

money, the body it assumes, the life it lives,
—our summer would have been full of industry and honour. How could Krupp hate the
men who are doing his will in massive iron?
How could Field hate the men who were
laying his cable in the ocean? The Church
must help stamp all our industrial falsehoods
into the dust, and must wave over all men
the flag of brotherhood.

So rapidly has friendship grown between
capital and labour, that a law is now before
the British Parliament looking to a com-
pensation to each labourer or his family for
injuries the working man may have received
in the execution of his task. When passed,
this law will each year give ten millions of
dollars to the working class of the three
islands. This law is not coming from the
" club " or " gun," but from the Christianity
of England.

This new humane philosophy has counted
all the toilers who have been injured in their
toil. It saw fifty-seven men killed while
building the Forth bridge, and one hundred
and thirty die among the wheels and machines
used in digging the Manchester canal. This
new kindness has studied longer and found
that of each ten thousand men employed on

the railways, fourteen are killed in a year and eighty badly crippled. In the long past there was no love that counted these dead or injured men. A dead labourer was as a dead horse or a dead dog. The riots and destruction and barbarity of last July set back all this new friendship, and made brotherly love despair of the present and future. The Evil One hath done this. Endless abuse, endless complaint, endless violence, openly taught anarchy, have succeeded in making work the enemy of money. You can recall the Bible story of the person who came at night and sowed tares among the springing wheat.

The fact that the United States army had to hasten hither to save life and property cannot all be charged upon the immigrants in our land. We have of late years been producing a group of Americans who care nothing for right or wrong, and who have become the masters of all the forms of abuse and discontent. It is evident that the influx of anarchists ought to cease, but we must not forget the crop our Nation is growing out of its own soil. All the cities seem uniting to make law ridiculous. The alien who will sell his vote for a few shillings is not so low as the American who will prefer these votes to principles. The immigrant may act through the absence of patriotism for his new land, but the American acts through total depravity.

The foreigners are generally manipulated by political confidence men, who are home-made.

The general theme of this morning is too large for the narrow limits of an essay, but it is possible for us to feel that our great Christian organism ought to be applied, from these dark days onward, to the making of the Christlike character. The Church, Catholic and Protestant, has lived for all other causes; let it, at last, live for a high intelligence and for individual righteousness. Literature and science and the public press will help the Church. All these wide-open and anxious eyes must perceive clearly that our national and personal happiness must come from the study and obedience of that kind of ethics which became so brilliant in Palestine. Our Jewish friends need not call it Christian, and our rationalized minds need not call it Divine. What is desirable and essential is, that its spirit shall sweep over us. Called by any name, it is a perfect salvation for our country and for each soul.

The Message of David Swing

The time and money the Church has given
to a metaphysical inquiry and teaching have
been a total loss. In the great college
courses, there are studies in classic language,
and in high mathematics, that strengthen
the intellect; but no such virtue has ever
been found to flow from the theological
studies of the Church. For hundreds of
years the mind has found in these enigmas
its slow doctrine. There, thousands, even
millions, of thinkers have found their grave.
There, the colossal mind of even a Pascal
grew confused and weak. There, great men
have lost their blessed earth while they were
fighting over the incomprehensible. God
did not give man this globe that it might be
made a desert or a battle-field, but that it
might be made the great home of great men.

As often as creeds and dogmas have detached the mind from humanity, literature
and art and science have rushed in to save
the precious things of society. But these
agencies have done this only by carrying, in
prose and verse and science, the laws of love,
duty and justice, by delineating man as a
brother of all men and as a subject in the
mighty kingdom of law and love. In an
age and in a republic marked by an amazing

effort to turn all things, all days, all life, into gold, our pulpits must make a new effort to reveal and create man the spiritual being, man temperate, man studious, man a lover of justice, man the brother, man Christlike. The same science that is seeking and finding the sources of wealth, and that is filling the young mind with longings to become rich, can find and teach all the worth of man as a spiritual being, and can compel a great nation and a great manhood to spring up from the philosophy of the soul.

To reach a result so new and so great, the pulpit must select new themes. It must cull them from the field where the mob raves, from the shops where men labour, from the poverty in which many die, from the office where wealth counts its millions. Even so beclouded a pagan as Virgil sang that when the mob is throwing stones and firebrands, and is receiving weapons from its fury, if Wisdom will only become visible and speak to it, it will listen, and at last obey. We have the mob; it is high time for a divine Wisdom to speak to it.

Our planet not only rolls on in the embrace of the laws of gravitation, of light and heat, vegetable and animal life, and the strange encompassment of the electric ether, but it flies onward amid spiritual laws far more wonderful—laws of labour and rest, laws of mental and moral progress, laws of perfect justice and of universal love. Oh, that God, by His almighty power, may hold back our Nation from destruction for a few more perilous years, that it may learn where lie the paths, in which, as brothers just and loving, all may walk to the most of excellence and the most of happiness !

Addresses and Papers
Foreign

X

A ROMAN HOME

A Letter to his Friend Ximines, from Tiro, a Slave of Cicero [1]

DEAR XIMINES :

I am still near the spot where my master was murdered. I am in his deserted library, and from a place so full of sacred memory, I must now write to you a long letter with the long-promised grave and light particulars about this greatest of the Romans. As though you were a woman, you beg to know all about the house and the wife and the children, and even the table and the entire private life of this orator. The wish is

[1] Marcus Tullius Tiro, a Greek slave belonging to Cicero. He was made a freedman, and was Cicero's librarian and amanuensis. He is believed to have much improved the art of stenography. This imaginary letter, while quoting from genuine " Familiar Epistles " of Cicero, is supposed to have been written by Tiro to his friend Ximines. It gives graphic details of Roman customs, and much concerning the life and death of the great orator, who was killed December 7, 43 B. C.

well enough ; because you can thus compare
Rome with Athens. Your wish shall be
gratified in part, for the cruel death of my
kind master only last week renders sacred
even the small things that now come up to
notice or to memory. Even this double ink-
stand, with black ink in one side and red in
the other, recalls the dead, for it is the very
one which my Cicero shook up when he said
he must write more distinctly to his brother
Quintus.

Does it seem so to you?—but I have indeed been the secretary and librarian of this
Roman for twenty years. You remember
that when I was a mere lad in Athens and
was being taught the two great languages
and all letters that I might be a literary
slave to some of the Athenians, Cicero, who
was then in our city to study rhetoric with
old Demetrius, formed quite an attachment to
me, and hoped to call me some day to Rome.
Twenty years have now passed since he sent
for me and paid my former master a large
sum for his literary slave, Tiro.

That you may know how light my bondage
for these years has been, and how well quali-
fied I am to speak about his domestic life, I
must insert an extract here from the almost

daily letters which Cicero sent me when he
was absent, and when I was sick at Tusculum.

" I did not imagine, dear Tiro, that I should
have been so little able to bear your absence,
but indeed it is almost beyond endurance.
Should you embark immediately you would
overtake me at Leucas. But if you are in-
clined to defer your voyage till your recovery
shall be more confirmed, let me entreat you
to be careful in selecting a safe ship, and be
careful that you sail in good weather, and
not without a convoy. It is true I am ex-
tremely desirous of your company, and as
early as possible, but the same affection which
makes me wish to see you soon makes me
wish to see you well."

And I must add here, lest I forget it, that
my master never struck me nor scolded me,
nor did he ever treat any of his slaves with
any cruelty. Some of the Romans do indeed
abuse their servants, and one matron recently
ordered one of her dressing maids put to
death because she arranged badly, or made
some error in the toilet of her mistress; but
I never saw any such inhumanity in the house
of my great master. I must insert here an
extract from another letter:

"I dispatched a letter to you from this place yesterday, where I continued all day waiting for my brother, and this I write just as we are setting out, and before sunrise. If you have any regard for us, but particularly for me, show it by your care to reëstablish your health. It is with great impatience I expect to meet you at Leucas; but if that cannot be, my next wish is that I may find Mario there with a letter. We all, but more particularly I myself, long to see you; however, we would by no means, dear Tiro, indulge ourselves in that pleasure unless it may be consistent with your health. I can forego your assistance, but your health, my dear Tiro, I would love to see restored, partly for your own sake—partly for mine. Farewell.

"*Alyzia, Nov., 5 A. M., 703 A. U. C.*"

Such kind letters he continually wrote me, and so many, that now I have quite a number of them, and how valuable they are, since they make me feel not that I passed long years of painful servitude with such a man, but instead, long years of elevating companionship.

When coming hither, so many years ago, on reaching the harbour nearest the Formian Villa, I found on the shore quite a crowd of people and an assortment of conveyances, much like those we have at home; there

were carriages for those who had furthest to
go ; there were litters for those who lived
only a few stadia over the hills. I inquired
for the house of Cicero, and was pointed to a
man as being the good Roman himself. In
a plain but elegant litter sat my future master. In another elegant one with embroid-
ered curtains sat his wife Terentia Cicero,
and the little daughter Tullia. These litters
were resting on their wooden braces, while
the sixteen slaves, whose business it was to
carry them, were lounging around in the sun,
almost every one of them having his hand
full of ripe figs at which he was munching
cheerfully. Cicero had come partly to meet
me, but partly from the custom the rich families have of going to the harbour, when they
see a vessel coming in. This great Roman
Demosthenes seemed glad to meet me, and as
we went home, I walked alongside his litter,
and as the curtains were looped up, he talked
all the while in a most elegant manner. He
found me quite familiar with recent and old
books, and at each discovery that I could
speak both Latin and Greek correctly, his
face brightened.

I then thought him a very homely man.
He was thin and pale, and his neck was very

long. When he reached over the rail to look forward or back, his neck seemed long as that of a crane. But amid the beauty of his character, the plainness of his person passed away. Terentia seemed cold and unbending and did not so much as speak to me, but Tullia, the little daughter, called out to me to ask if I would not help her get out her lessons in Greek.

Did you know, Ximines, that the wealthy Romans do not limit themselves to one country place? In addition to a costly city residence, my master had fourteen villas for his summer or winter pleasure. Wherever an island or a harbour or a hill especially pleased him, he bought or built a house, and several places were given him by wealthy friends, who were or might be his clients in law, or who were moved by simple friendship. Many large sums were given to this lawyer in the wills of those who had been near him in life.

Happy summers we spent sailing or journeying to and fro among these beautiful places of rest. The Tusculum Villa was the favourite of us all, and the chief of the group. It was in the border of Rome. From it we could see all the public buildings in the one direction and all the beauty of hill and vale

and water and sky in another. Here were
our library, our pictures, our statuary, our
best gardens and fields, our fowls, geese,
ducks, pheasants, peacocks and pigeons. My
master's city residence was costly, and was
wonderful in its ornaments and apartments,
but we all loved more the resort out at Tusculum. That city home, Clodius, the consul,
in the depth of malice, ordered to be razed
to the ground when he banished Cicero. For
days the mob and also the better people could
be seen carrying off fragments or ornaments
or plunder from that overthrown palace.
But a change of consuls soon came and
Rome recalled the exile and rebuilt our city
house.

Our Tusculum villa is built much like a
general's camp, the soul being in the centre,
the body, the impedimenta, being located all
around the valuable part. The main hall of
the villa is the soul. Here is the conversation, here the beauty, here the feast, here the
art, here the whole family. All around are
the shops and sleeping bunks of the servants.
This villa is approached through a long lane
of dwarf box. This accommodating shrub is
trimmed and bent into the shapes of animals
in a pretty or grotesque manner. Rampant

lions and the panther so much seen in the games, the peacock and other birds, are on either hand as you approach the main entrance of the house. The structure measures about a hundred feet across the front and extends back fully two hundred feet. The exterior is set apart for rooms for the artisan slaves. Our carpenter has one, our tailor one, our groom one, our cook one, and thus on until the family is in the midst of quite an army of these domestic troops. Like almost all the Roman houses it is built of brick, but some parts of it are lined with marble. But Rome is a brick city, the bricks being about one span square.

Entering this large square by a beautiful gate, you are passed inward by the keepers, and after a few steps you come into the great hall, which is the home of the Cicero family. Marble columns support the roof, which is raised high above the head. Marble is under foot. All around one stands statuary, most of which come from Greek towns. The side walls are made of stucco, and these are exquisitely painted. To the height of a man above the floor, the colours are dark, and the figures are set ones, but above that the colours are very bright and the figures either perfect vines and flowers, or else images of human and divine ideals. In this immense room we ate and talked, and played and laughed, and gave parties, and danced and were happy, until death entered the gate to break up this island of the blessed. In some Roman houses in the city there are steps to lead up to a second story, but this is rarely the case. The bedchambers are recesses from the great hall and sometimes there is one sleeping berth above another, and the one who sleeps above climbs up by two pins inserted in the masonry.

At Tusculum, my master had a bedroom made for himself in the rear of the building. He had ordered deadened walls on all sides, and a window that he could darken; that when he had been up late at night he might not be disturbed by that clatter of all kinds made by the slaves, nor be awakened by the too obtrusive sunshine of the morning.

The library was a room with the walls on all sides arranged for books. Each book had its little cell, like the holes in which our pigeons live. It was not my place to take care of the volumes, but to read them to my master and to his family and friends; and to be forever seeking for new truths or ideas or beauties for the great orator's happiness and use. He had a slave who looked after the binding and dusting and arranging of the works. Cicero would not permit a dirty cover to remain on a volume, nor a soiled label. All must be bright and cheerful, much as the good man was himself. One set of books he had such as I never saw at Athens —books full of portraits. He had seven hundred portraits of distinguished Romans. As Brutus and Cæsar had the same pictures in their libraries, I concluded and heard that there was some shop where one picture could be multiplied until all could have copies; but I have not yet found that ingenious shop.

Our library is ornamented in fine manner by paintings and statuary. Now I remember how mad my master was, when, having ordered Atticus to buy him some good pieces in Greece, that erring friend shipped to us a lot of cupids and nymphs. My master did not want such stuff in his rooms.

Passing out of the library, one comes to the flower-garden and fish-ponds and poultry-yard. How much that great Cicero did love his geese and peacocks and chickens and pigeons! Even when he knew he must make an important speech that day, and

when he was full of care about the oration,
he would yet take the time in the morning
to go out and see how the pigeons and
pheasants were getting along. I have known
him to pay a large sum for two pigeons'
eggs that he heard would hatch out some
rare species. In the flower-garden and
among the fruit trees, the dinner and supper
were often served in the summer months. I
often read aloud while the family ate. I
loved thus to read, for the grass under foot
secured for us such a silence that reading and
hearing were more delightful.

Permit me now to rest you a little, dear
Ximines, by leading you from the small to
the great, for you know, dear friend, the
soul is so constructed that it can find rest in
going from the little to the large, or from
the large to the little. Man can walk a
circle with less fatigue if at times he changes
his direction. Let me tell you about Cicero
as a student and an orator. He was wider
in his tastes than our Demosthenes. You
know our orator loved only matters of State,
but this Roman loved all books and all
things. He read everything he could find.
If I found a good passage I went to him
with it, perfectly assured that he would en-

joy it whether it was prose or poetry, or law or religion or geography, or only a piece for exciting laughter. In one way or another, all he saw or heard or read, helped him in either his public speeches or his conversations. All that went into his brain came out again in some better shape.

He will live in the world's fame as an orator, but I shall remember with deepest pleasure his fun and talk at home. Every evening friends came in. There were Trebatius and Hortensius and Atticus and Rufus and Brutus and Cato, and by degrees my master would become aroused, and all evening long he would pour forth jokes and anecdotes or else would quote gems from the poets. He was a mimic of manners, and would keep all delighted by mimicking all the bad and eccentric speakers of the city and the clowns of the day. Grave as my master was in his public addresses, he filled some of his letters to friends and sometimes the rooms of justice and always our home, with sayings that led to much laughter and much good cheer. In all the letters he wrote to the young lawyer, Trebatius, who had gone with Cæsar on his British expedition, there were seldom any words except those of pure humour. He expressed in one of them the opinion that his friend had gone over the sea, that he might be the greatest lawyer now living in Britain. In another he opines that the reason why his friend had remained carefully away from battle could not be found in any cowardice, but it must have been in the unwillingness of a student of law to be guilty of making an assault. In one of the replies of Trebatius, there were signs that some former writing had been erased to leave the page blank for the letter to Cicero. In the next missile to this absent friend, Cicero expressed a wonder what could have been on that paper that could have made it less valuable than the proposed letter—he concluded that what was erased "must have been one of your own [Trebatius'] briefs."

When Verres was upon trial for defrauding the people of Sicily, for stealing statuary and jewels and pictures, and for assessing and collecting most unjust taxes, Hortensius defended, and Cicero prosecuted the accused. It was known to my master that Verres had sent to his attorney a valuable piece of marble—an Egyptian Sphinx. In the course of the examination of witnesses, Hortensius became angry at one of those on the side of

the prosecution, and thundered out that he
wanted no riddles but a plain statement of
facts. Cicero said calmly, " Hortensius, you
should be glad to get a supply of riddles
since you have at home such a valuable
sphynx." This quite upset the gravity of
the crowd, and all laughed over the predica-
ment of the distinguished Hortensius.

There was a form of literary sport which
was my master's great delight—a double use
of a word ; a use in which the hidden import
would suddenly spring up, bringing always
a pleasure. These double-edged words he
loved to send off to this same fun-loving
Trebatius. He reminded him that the win-
ters would be cold up in Gaul, but that his
regimentals, when they should come, would
keep out much cold ; and that Cæsar would
perhaps have some hot work for him ; and
that upon the whole he was not so hopeless
as a soldier as he was as a lawyer. Trebatius
having remained on the peaceful side of a
river while Cæsar went over to fight, Cicero
congratulated the friend that he had so far
eliminated all ill-will from his heart that he
had become unwilling even to cross water ! ! !

Indeed I shall not deny that to see the
housetops covered with people and the streets

densely crowded with a multitude, all silent
to hear Cicero speak against the cruel Verres,
or the despot Antony, was a great spectacle
and one which it was my fortune often to
witness, but, for some reason, my own memory will cherish most those evenings in the
villas when the jokes were so good and all
were so perfectly happy. Julius Cæsar at
one time determined to gather up in a little
volume all the Cicero stories and witticisms
he could find, but I fear that the last five
years of Cæsar's life were passed in so much
war and turmoil that he never prosecuted
his intention. At none of the bookstores do
I find any such volume. I need no such
volume, but the laughing world will.

My master spoke much like the orators
we have seen and heard in Athens. He imi-
tated and he acted as he spoke. He threw
himself about from place to place on the
rostrum and seemed to have in him the souls
of a whole company of men. When he first
began speaking in public, he was so full of
action and passion that he injured his health
and was compelled to leave Rome and seek
peace abroad. He spoke just as do the actors in the theatres, changing his face and
voice to suit each style of the changing

thought and argument. He had an extreme ambition and seemed to know in youth that he was destined to be great. When he entered the law some wanted him to change his name, for Cicero meant only a vegetable. They told him it did not sound large enough. He said in reply that he would keep his father's name and make it sound honourable. He wore out his health in a few years and sailed to Greece for rest. On his return, he assumed a manner a little more quiet but it was still very full of action. But, my good friend, he was a wonderful man. I always attended him when he was to make a speech that when he came to write it out fully afterwards, I could aid him if he had lost any particular thought or the structure of a sentence. I have known the lawyers opposed in a case to my master to venture no reply but to abandon their cause after Cicero had made his opening speech.

A rather amusing event took place while Cæsar was dictator, only a few years ago. A case was before Cæsar. The evidence having been all taken, Cæsar was about to give his judgmen* and had declared that no speeches need be made as his mind had been made up fully that the person charged was guilty. Cicero arose to make a brief voluntary plea. Cæsar said jokingly that he had not heard Cicero for so long that it would be rather pleasant to hear the good fellow speak once again. He heard him; got amazed and highly wrought up, and discharged the accused as being the most innocent man of his acquaintance.

Ah, my Ximines, let me tell you more now of the home life of the dead orator and master, more dear to me as a master than as an orator. Let me tell you briefly about the social scenes in our city house, and also in the villa at Tusculum. One of our largest reunions of friends was given when Cicero's only daughter Tullia had just begun to attract the attentions of Roman lovers. As soon as night had fully come the friends began to pour in. Some came by carriages, some by the popular litter. At last you could have seen gathered in the hall Julius Cæsar and his wife; Decimus Brutus and Marcus Brutus, Cato, Hortensius, Marcus Antony, Crassus, Quintus Cicero, the brother of my Marcus, Pompey and Publius, Crassus Atticus, Casca, and a hundred other such notable men. Not any less was the number of the noble women and maidens. Pomponia,

the wife of Cicero's brother, came early and
had begun to chat with her sister-in-law.
Cornelia, the daughter of Metellus Scipio,
was there dressed in plain, but rich costume,
for she was a woman of intellect rather than
of dress. She resembled the Cornelia of
Gracchi fame. The Lælia girls were present in all their style of costume and beauty
of face. There were three of them, and
they might have stood for three Graces. The
talk that Cicero thought too highly of these
daughters was all old time gossip.

In this throng were not a few of the
Roman "pretty men," *homo bellus*. The
bellus homo is a man wholly devoted to
fashion and dress and pleasure. The number
of these has greatly increased of late years.
The young men in general seem to be of
this sleek and effeminate school. The sons
of the great senators and orators are for
the most part idle, pretty men, who part
their hair with the utmost precision and
smell of all the perfumes of the South. They
wear snow-white robes, and powder like
women to make white their bare arms ; and
in the wearing of rings they equal any
matron of this dying Republic. These
youths gathered that night in one corner of

the great hall, and with a few equally silly
girls they hummed over part of Nile love-
songs, and lounged in the large soft seats de-
signed for the ladies of rank.

Most of the love-songs here locate their
scenes of romance and the actors in the
scenes over on the Nile; not only because
Cleopatra has introduced there an era of
sentiment, but rather because the spirit of
romance always finds its ideal land away
from home, there being no witchery in
things that are near. I remember that we
boys at Athens sang of Roman adventure,
but coming hither I found the Roman young
souls locating the exploits of successful and
unsuccessful love as far as possible away
from all existing realities. It must belong
to human nature to cover up with enchant-
ment hills and vales and peoples that are
just beyond the eye's field of vision.

At times I heard some elegant measures
from some thoughtful poet, but for the most
part these brainless youths sang little verses
of which I may give you here a fair sample:

> If you would live your life
>   In the light of woman's smile,
> And escape all toil and strife,
>   Then away to the Nile!

There my barge may float all night
  On the love-creating stream,
Where the soft and amber light
  Changes life into a dream.

My love is in the boat
  And I am by her side ;
Oh, let me ever float
  On this love-producing tide.

In Rome at all hours of the night one can hear some part of this shape of song rising up from the streets, and so fully alive is the whole city to the romance of love affairs, that even old men whistle these tunes as they plod along to work or to idleness, generally to idleness, for none but slaves pursue any toilsome occupation.

Of this trifling class was Cicero's son Marcus. At least, while he was away in Greece at school, word often came to us that he was living in a dissipated manner and was spending much more money than had been allowed him. But not of this foolish class was the daughter Tullia. She resembled her father in her love of learning and of wise conversation, and thus when our parties were given this beautiful girl was found talking with Cæsar or Pollio or Archias, rather than with the fops at the other end of

the corridor. Had I not been only a servant,
it would have been an immeasurable joy
could I have sought and gained her love.
As things were, I confess, my dear Ximines,
my heart beat quickly with happiness when
she would request me to bring her a certain
volume and read for the company, at her
command, some sentiment that had given her
delight. My partiality, perhaps, made me
admire her dress more than the magnificent
toilet of Cæsar's wife or the gay attire of
the Lælia daughters. On this particular
evening Tullia wore over her wine-coloured
dress a delicately tinted pink scarf which
quite enfolded her. It had a still brighter
border. Her hair was heaped up rather
negligently on her head, and was held in
place by a gold arrow. As she played on
the harp and sang, she showed a sandal with
a rim of gold all around the sole, and a perfect network of pearls covering the instep of
her almost sacred foot. Add to these ornaments a golden ball which she would at
times toss to some, and from which would
gush forth a little cloud of perfumed dust,
and you can see this loved and now wept-for
Tullia. I used to wonder what the great
father would have said or done had I ever

taken by the hand that beautiful being, or had I ever addressed a note of affection to her. Now that both are dead I am glad that my insane love never ventured forth in formal language.

On this evening we had for the feast all the fish and fowls and fruits known to Roman or Greek, and the most elegant wines. Cicero loved glassware with quite a passion, and his engraved goblets were passed freely about, filled with their nectar of Bacchus. Cæsar, the most distinguished of our guests, ate but little, but you should have seen him eat once at our Formian [1] house. He announced that he was intending to have a full feast, and feast he did, for he intended on rising from dinner to take an emetic, and spare himself the pain of digesting such a load of meat and fruit and wine. You know the feast-goers often do this—eat all they can, with the intention of taking, after the meal, this "emetikon." The gluttons do it, not that they may escape distress, but that they may return and eat a second dinner the same night. They create a stomach like that of the vulture, which can load and unload almost at pleasure.

[1] This villa of Cicero's was in Formiæ, Italy.

For another reason Cæsar's visit to our Formian village was remarkable, for he brought with him a thousand men, soldiers and friends. Most of them encamped in the garden, but my master had to feed all outside the environs and to entertain the important men of the number within the walls, and they ate and drank in a most hearty manner. Next day, when the company had departed to the last man, Cicero came up to me in the library, and remarked, with a grave face: "Cæsar is indeed a very notable guest, but he is not one of those fellows to whom, on his going, one says, 'Call again.'"

My master was no feasting man. There were only a few simple things he could eat. No fish or oyster could he digest, and even after all the care he took of his health he suffered all the years I was with him. He drank wine, but seldom to excess. Only one night is recalled now when he came home with his intellect clouded by wine. He had been out spending the evening with two fellow lawyers, and coming home about midnight he did not as usual come into the library, but he passed straight to his room. In the morning he mentioned, with regret, that he feared he had drank so much the night

before as to expel his wits, for his companions had asked him for an opinion of a
law point and he now felt that he had
given a foolish reply. On consulting the
reports I found that my master had not
been very drunk after all. The question
that had been raised at the neighbour's was,
whether an heir to an estate could bring
action for damages the estate had sustained
before it actually came into his possession,
he being the legal heir apparent?

My dear Ximines, I must give you rest from
these small matters, by telling you now in
rapid succession of four large events; I may
call them the four dark days of all the long
years. In their books the Egyptians and the
Persians tell of days when the sun did not
shine, but showed a black, sullen face; when
the wild bird flew to its nest, and the cattle
bellowed and groaned in the fields. Be these
stories true or not, dark days came to our
house. First came the divorce of the wife
and mother, Terentia. On a certain day,
only five years ago, this wife and mother
bade Tullia farewell, and left the home
where she had been through all the period
of her girlhood and middle life. I saw little
reason for such a crisis in the house. I am

positive that the event came so gradually that all the parties—the husband and wife and daughter—were already reconciled to it when it came really to pass. My master had had many great trials, and under them was growing old. He needed perfect peace in his home, and constant praise from all. Terentia managed badly all the money matters. She never praised in any manner her famous husband : but on the opposite, set up an opposition of feeling, if I may so speak. Cicero was himself so great that he filled the house to such a degree that there was no room for another. Tullia was full of demonstration over all her father's speeches and writings ; and as she drew ever nearer her father, the mother to that degree receded. By degrees Terentia began to look away towards the house of her own father as offering her an asylum, and with the large dowry handed back to her, which she had brought Cicero in her youth, she went away from our villas forever. It is a good quality of Roman law that a man who puts aside his wife must first restore to her the dowry she brought him in her days of youth and beauty. She could not come rich and go away poor.

No sooner had our home circle recovered from this calamity than there came the greatest one that could have assailed the tender heart of my master. Tullia suddenly died. In about her twentieth year, this daughter, whom he had called the "honey sweet," took away from earth her blessed face and language.

She had been married, but yet her father's home was almost all the time cheered by her presence; and when the word came from her sick room that the disease had become suddenly alarming, the grief of the illustrious father was most extreme. Death came very suddenly. All the deep philosophy of my master failed him. Letters from all the great men of the land came to him, bearing all forms of consolation, and some full of reproof that such a statesman should be so broken down by the death of only a daughter. But letters brought no softening of the affliction. We withdrew to our villa of Astura, because, being upon an island, it offered the broken heart two blessings—security against the intrusion of man, and the presence of all the sweetness of nature. Here, in this lonely place, my master did not even desire my presence any longer, but alone, every morning, he would walk away to the woods, and would not, perhaps, until evening emerge from their sympathetic shadows. He was also alone much in his library, and, entering it in his absence, I would find on his table outlines of monuments and forms of epitaphs. His heart, unable any longer to look forward, was thus looking back. Life has been awfully injured when it looks only back.

The tragic fate of Cæsar soon followed, to conceal the tomb of the "honey sweet daughter." All the patriots, and all the rivals of Cæsar, too, had feared that the Ides of March would see him declared king. The friends of this royal movement had pretended to find oracular dictates that only a king could conquer the Parthians. As the Ides drew near, the city became restless and suspicious in all ways at once. On the morning of the Ides we all went to the Senate. By noon Cicero and I, his servant, were in our places, anxious, but uncertain. My master knew of no conspiracy. All began to wonder that Cæsar did not come to preside, for there seemed to be business awaiting transaction. I learned that night that Cæsar had resolved, as by mere accident, to stay at home until the much talked of Ides should have passed by.

That morning his wife had told him that she had dreamed that he had come flying to her in the night, saying, " Save me ! " This helped detain Cæsar. He had also gone out in the garden in the morning to note how his doves and pheasants would fly when he should feed them or call them. They came up on his left hand. This also helped him in his resolution to let that day pass by in the most possible of retirement. The conspirators, finding the day passing and that their victim would perhaps not come to the forum, made out a pressing demand for the imaginary king, and sent down a messenger to Cæsar's house, telling him that a case of importance was being argued, and that the Senate would be gratified if he would come and preside. He at once dismissed his secret forebodings, and ordering out his litter, entered and was borne along to the assembly. To a watchman on the street he remarked pleasantly : " Ah, friend, the Ides of March have come, and have brought no trouble." " Come, but not gone ! " was the reply.

Seated upon his Chair of State in the Curia Pompeii, Cæsar asked that the case be at once presented. Tullius Cimber then said that he had a brother in exile whom he would now petition the Senate to recall; and while pleading for this brother he grew more and more earnest, and at the end of each sentence took a step forward as though he would lay his affectionate pleadings upon the very breast of Julius. Other senators, too, began to speak as though the case were one of tremendous importance; and as they spoke they, too, moved gently forward. It is my own impression, dear Ximines, that they overdid their earnestness, and that Cæsar's heart suddenly divined that the eloquence was full of something more terrible than the exile of Cimber's brother. Cæsar arose from his seat, but in an instant the dagger of Casca gleamed and came down. I heard the dead sound of the blow. In his fearful tremulousness Casca had struck his grand victim only in the shoulder-blade. Cæsar grasped the dagger, and screamed forth in a loud voice, "Casca, you villain, what means this?" While we all gazed, horror-stricken, suddenly other daggers gleamed and struck, and the great man, muttering some pathetic words which I could not catch, fell heavily upon the floor. Some relate that he said, "And thou, Brutus!" Others told me next day that when he saw Brutus raise his dagger, he said, "And my son! Brutus!" It had long been rumoured that Brutus was a son of Cæsar.

In a few days after this thrilling event, my master began to say that it was a great oversight in the Republicans not to have slain Antony; that he was more willing to be a despot than Julius had been, and that had the conspirators invited him (Cicero) to their liberty feast, there was one dish that would not have been carried away uncarved. My master despised and feared Mark Antony. I must close this letter, dear Ximines, by telling you how this enmity soon hurried my Cicero out of life. When Antony and Octavius and Lepidus formed the second Triumvirate, and deceived the people by giving them three tyrants instead of one, each two of the Triumvirs conceded to the other the privilege of putting to death his greatest enemy. Lepidus demanded Lucius Cæsar; Octavius demanded Paulus; Antony asked the life of Cicero.

We were at the Tusculum villa. A messenger came in fearful haste, his horse almost falling from fatigue. Cicero and his brother went out to meet him, and in a few moments came back into the great hall. Cicero said

to me, calmly : " Antony has condemned me
to death." My heart sunk. I was in a moment glad that Tullia had passed to the
grave, which has no fresh sorrow. A group
of servants were called, both boatmen and
porters, and, having gotten ready the most
essential things, we hurried to Astura, one
of my master's villas, a few stadia away.
Should we reach that point, from there we
should sail for Macedonia. But there was
little hope of a final escape from the wide
domain of Rome. The road was literally
sprinkled with our tears. When we halted,
each stood with an arm around his friend,
and Cicero and his brother embraced each
other many times, and bade many farewells ;
for, in my master, friendship was as vast a
thing as learning or eloquence.

We sailed from Astura, but, after a day
out in tough weather, Cicero grew sick, and
at the same time he felt a great longing to
risk his native land, or die upon its soil. He
made our seamen sail into a harbour where
we had a villa, and there we all disembarked.
The porters took up the litter and bore him
to our beautiful Formian house. Here we
had known happy times in the past. When
we had gotten into the ample hall, he said,

"Let me die here, in the country I have attempted so often to save."

He lay down to sleep. It was the 7th of December. In only a few moments, servants came in from remote parts of the farm, saying that horsemen were coming towards the house. The porters did not wait for the order or even the permission of Cicero, but, affectionately taking him up, they laid him in the litter, and told him they must go back to the ship. We had advanced only a hundred paces when the assassins closed up around the baffled group. The slaves set down the litter. Cicero parted the curtains, and reaching out his head, gray with age and trouble, he addressed one of the pursuers by name, and said: "Strike me, if you think it is right." The bloody men halted an instant. The face before them was calm and noble. The hearts, conscious of guilt, faltered, but only for an instant. Herrennius, who had dismounted, stepped forward, and, with a half dozen ill-aimed and cruel blows, he severed the head from the body. The body remained in the litter; the head rolled over on the earth beneath. The hands, too, were cut off and were borne to Antony, who ordered them to be fastened up in the Forum, where the lips and hands, too, had been so eloquent against kings.

My dear Ximines, I heard this matchless speaker deliver more than thirty great orations, and I have read all his books and letters, and am thus familiar with the utterances, public and private, of his great soul, but, to my memory, no words of his come now with more significance or beauty than those uttered in the last days of his life : " I try to make my enmities transient, and my friendships eternal."

Your friend,

TIRO.

Tusculum Villa, Dec. 19, A. U. C. 710.
[The year 43 B. C.]

XI

DANTE[1]

EACH myth is probably believed by the
tribes which first utter it. Children
are often six or seven years old before they
turn away from the realism of Santa Claus
and his sleigh, but no lapse of years can turn
the mind away from Santa Claus as a symbol. To us who are oldest the myth is just
as valuable as it was when it was not a myth
but a truth to the mind of our childhood.
By the time a race has reached the power to
produce a literature it has passed the period
of belief in its own wonderland. What was
once true turns into mental furniture, ornament, available capital, a pictorial language.
We Americans have just as much use for
Hercules as Virgil had, because the story enables us to express the difficulty of cleaning
the Augæan stables of a city, and to slay that
Lernæan Hydra which infests each metrop-
olis of the American Occident and Orient.

[1] Born in May, 1261 ; died September 14, 1321 A. D.

It is impossible to learn now how much Homer believed of his own tale, but it seems almost certain that he dealt with the dog Kerberus just as the Egyptians had used the animal before Homer and exactly as our Milton made use of the Hell Hound in recent years.

Some Greek realist of the Socratic period said that Homer ought to be removed from Greek thought, because he taught the people a mass of fables; but the human family has not regarded the suggestion, for fables are what we all want. We do not feel them as truth, but as powerful illustrations of truth. We want them as language. We do not want Lot's wife as a pillar of salt, but we do desire to keep in mind that if an educated and beautiful woman starts towards some noble life and then concludes after all that she would rather dance and sing in a basement saloon, she ought to be smitten into some insensate stick, stock or stone. Her life possesses no value.

It seems just to Dante to look upon him as making that use of the wonderful to which Virgil and Ovid had subjected it, but only for nobler purposes—for the decorations of a higher theme. Milton did not believe in

233

any of his details, but we all come from the " Paradise Lost " with the simple feeling that we have for hours and hours been in a world above and beyond our setting sun.

When Dante finds a group of souls existing in the form of trees of which the leaves sigh in eternal sorrow and drip with a bloody dew, he simply borrows from Ovid, and especially from Virgil, whose companions in attempting to pull up a shrub are amazed to hear its roots cry out : " Do not lacerate me thus, for I am Polydorus." To Dante's living human trees are added as appropriate birds the Harpies which had figured at the camp of Æneas.

Each writer in each successive period becomes heir to an enormous lot of images and pictures which become his language. The personal relation of Virgil to his myths was that of Goethe to his Faust, and of Milton towards his Satan, and of Klopstock towards his elegant angel Ithuriel. Mr. Hamilton Mabie delineates in one of his books some mysterious movements on the part of Nature. The winds, the black clouds, had been angry for many hours ; they had in some manner impressed the lightning and thunder into the atmospheric misunderstanding ; great

volumes of blackness had been flung at the
sun by day and into the face of the moon at
night. The unpleasantness was all a mystery
until daylight having come, our friend threw
open his shutter and saw the apple trees in full
bloom. We now dismiss all the intellectual
machinery of which the writer made use and
simply thank him for dispelling our stupidity
and coaxing us to look at a blossoming
orchard. He did not believe in any quarrel
in the upper air. Thus Homer, Virgil, Dante,
Milton and Shakespeare are all practical
common-sense men, but they are rich in
intellectual furniture. Their ability to put a
truth on a stage was wonderful. But Dante
and Beatrice are not a piece of absolute
realism. The sweet girl was much more
loved than many, but so was Virgil a favourite
of Dante. Beatrice was simply the one
blossom, highest and reddest, of a luxuriant
soul. Virgil, Statius, Rachel and Matilda
all share with Beatrice in this outpoured
love in Dante's great work.

Dante was nearly forty years old when he
toiled at the production of the now illustrious
poem. He was about thirty years distant
from that boyhood morning in which he
looked with such rapture upon the child

Beatrice. Whatever may have been the dazzle of those youthful days, nearly all thoughtful persons who live in this century cannot but feel that that romance of the tenth year could have reached the fortieth only in the form of a beautiful memory. Romantic love is one of those small boats which, although magnificent as the barge of Cleopatra, is better for a coast service than for crossing the wide sea. Thirty years are too wide an ocean; Dante's bannered barge did not cross it. But there is an event that is common—that of a sensitive and noble mind looking back and bedecking with new tears the object it kissed long ago. When cares and misfortunes have been many, and when the future becomes too small to contain much of hope, the past all reopens and the heart arises and says: I will go back to my father's house. There love and plenty await me. The more husks and swine about the feet, the more willing and grand is the return.

It is quite unjust to Dante to think of him as " the lover sighing like a furnace, with a woeful ballad made to his mistress' eyebrow ; " for although he did inscribe a mighty sonnet to the eyes of his mistress, he must be granted the credit of having waited until the love which came at first sight had been subdued by all the worldly events of more than thirty years. He was, indeed, wonderfully sentimental, but he was also a soldier, a statesman, a scholar. Beatrice was only a colour thrown over a varied life like the colour of a sunset, whose hues turn sky, land and trees, living or dead, into pure gold. But there was nothing of the weak young man in the nature of Dante. His era was romantic. To be in love was the privilege of each separate person ; and so open-hearted were the Italians that the new or the old attachments of each one were matters of confession and common conversation equalled in our day by the themes of science or politics.

Dante and Beatrice were parallelled in the lives of many men and women of those intermediate centuries. The Minnesingers and the errant knights had made song and love rank as fine arts. It was the wonderful prevalence and power of love-song that induced Dante to break friendship with the Latin language and utter his soul in the current words of the people. He wrote the first part of the "Inferno" in the classic tongue, but in the years in which that manuscript was resting he reached some new appreciation of the popular speech, and when he resumed the comedy the thoughts ran out in harmonious Italian. It is probable that the Latin tongue had become so associated with the law and theology of the age that it seemed unable to be the accompaniment of the song the poet intended to sing. Language, like all other objects, is liable to become the victim of associations. The same sentimentalism which exalted Beatrice exalted the Italian dialect. The language of his love overpowered the language of his theology.

Admitting that all the fashionable people of that period made romantic love a channel and expression of culture, we must concede that Dante possessed a poetic sensibility which made him almost outdo his own age. Whatever may be the genius of a time, there will be leaders in the dominant pursuit or condition. If the age be scientific, there will be Newtons; if it be philosophic, there will be Lockes and Hamiltons; if it be religious, there will be Xaviers and Marquettes. While, therefore, Dante loved according to the custom of his times, he was eminent in his department and no doubt surpassed the common crowd in a kind of adoration of persons. In our own times it is evident that John Stuart Mill, Henry Hallam, and Robert Browning were capable of carrying more than the common quantity of affection. The death of young Hallam, of Mrs. Mill, and of Mrs. Browning were shadows wonderfully deep in the hearts upon which they fell. Mill and Hallam never again saw earth in its old beauty. Those two graves made each sunset bring tears. Upon Dante there must be seen falling the full, rich untorn mantle of his country and epoch. In the midst of love he was above all; he was a dashing leader in the great battle-field of the heart.

The age which made this poet so romantic also transformed the adored child and woman. When a girl possessed great beauty and greatness of character, she became an emblem while she lived and almost a divinity after her death. The world was still so young and illogical, so wonder-loving, that it personified all spiritual beauties and virtues. The concrete was dearer than the abstract. The Greeks and Romans worshipped a little army of Minervas, Junos, Venuses, Dianas, and nymphs, because they did not respect the real

woman enough to tempt their hearts to make
for her a throne or a pedestal. Each Minerva
proclaimed the absence of the real woman.
When woman became great in learning or
talent she declined in morals, and Aspasia
and Cleopatra were so affected by gossip that
when men wished to worship womanhood
they turned towards Minerva rather than
towards the favourites of Pericles and Mark
Antony.

The invasion of the world by the New
Testament wrought a gradual but at last a
radical change. Those gospels and letters
chased the Venuses and Dianas out of art
and created a demand for such earthly sym-
bols as the Marys and the Magdalens. Ce-
cilia, Teresa, and quite a long roll of human
saints made the worship of Beatrice possible.
Much as the Protestants may be opposed to
the mariolatry of the Roman Catholics, they
should confess the services which the " Ave
Marias " have performed in behalf of womanhood. They have taken from the clouds, the
groves, the fountains and the sea the virtues
of a thousand nymphs and have conferred
them upon the terrestrial woman. John
Stuart Mill and his wife make up of womanhood a better picture for man than that of

Numa Pompilius and the goddess Egeria.
Since the Mary of Bethlehem came, humanity
has wasted less worship over the chimeras of
the childish ages. It has used all its intellect and sentiment in the upbuilding of the
kingdom of womanhood. It has not been
drained of wealth by a costly foreign policy.

To exchange the goddesses for womanhood
was not only what would seem a good form
of barter looked upon in any light, but it was
rendered more profitable to civilization by the
fact that the womanhood must be idealized in
order that the orators, poets and lovers could
pass from Diana to Mary, from a Juno to a
Beatrice. There must be some resemblance
between the old divine and the new human.
The Marys and Marthas were thus thrown
upward into a figure larger than the reality.
The New Testament so exalted the plane of
female life that it soon became very possible
to have in Rome or Florence human emblems
of a physical and moral beauty which had
always been supposed celestial. Olympus
was displaced by Florence.

It was in a climate full of the warmth of
nature, in an age of romance, in a time of
transition between the unreal and the real,
that the boy Dante met the girl of exceeding

beauty. That she was the loveliest creature of the times no one need deny. According to Carlyle, each generation contains its loveliest face as well as its worst book or meanest man. By very slow degrees Dante wove this loveliest face into his poems as a most fitting motive. Not only did he wait for the beauty to die and become an angel, but he had patiently and silently passed over the time and fact of her marriage. It was ten years after her death and about fourteen years after Dante's marriage to another woman, that his poems began to appear in the name of the infinite friendship.

It would thus seem that the poet in the noon of his sad experience, driven by his inward genius to hold up his generation to the gaze of the people, selected this dead and half-idolized beauty to be the motive of his long symphony.

Dante did not bear patiently his banishment. He made repeated attempts to get back to his city with its beauty and precious friendships, and at each failure his heart became more melancholy and his fury more flaming. The volume which slowly grew in his mind was not a simple poem, not a love-story. It was an encyclopædia of Italy.

Italy had been in a political turmoil for the several generations in which the two parties struggled for supremacy—the papal power and the temporal power—the former an absolute throne, the latter a constitutional monarchy. The papal party was founded upon miracles, the limited monarchists upon the history of Greek and Roman law. The struggle of those two ideas made Florence and Rome battle-grounds not only for swords but for words: and by the time Dante had drunk in a heart full of political wrongs and sorrows, he had in mind a large number of persons who ought to be thought of as in hell or purgatory, and his heart held a memory of many noble ones who ought to be dreamed of as in heaven.

The book was thus too great to be a love story ; it was intended to be the history of a period—a bar of judgment created as an outline of the final day of punishment and reward. If any persons now living should open the volume with the thought of finding in it any love-making, any rapturous kisses over proposal and acceptance, it is not in the power or extent of this essay to express the disappointment they will experience as they read ; but if any one loves to mark what political and religious ideas were moving slowly across the Eleventh, Twelfth, and Thirteenth Centuries, what silent formations as cloud and storm were reaching up in the sky, what rifts there were through which shone the sun, what kind of political leaders needed perdition, what kind of popes, cardinals and bishops needed the limbo of pain and regrets, what noble ideas had come down from the classics, what nobler ones from the simple truths of Palestine, what lofty beings had risen up in every age, what groupings of truths genius can make, what lofty decorations the art of literature can rear upon the thrilling or beautiful facts of our race, and how poetry can draw the truest portrait of history, to such a one the work named " Dante " will seem not a tale of romance but a vast stream of knowledge and eloquence.

Dante was not a Beau Brummell, nor an N. P. Willis. He was a heroic character, ready to be a soldier or an ardent student of Paris or Padua. He was once ruler in chief of the Principality of Florence ; a citizen king of the town that could grow such people as Beatrice. He was no languishing lover. He was rather a combination of part Pericles and part Homer. Beatrice was not a part of Dante's life, so much as a part of his literary art. In life, he loved her a little; in literature he loved her deeply.

Dante was the transition heart between the old poetic epic and the new era of novels. When the "Divine Comedy" was written, no novel had ever been composed. Had this Florentine lived six hundred years later, his beautiful girl would have become a Mrs. Robert Ellsmere, and Dante's scorn would have missed the Pope and smitten John Calvin and modern Orthodoxy. But fortunately for us, in the Thirteenth Century the novel had not yet been invented.

What is a novel? Literature in general is that part of the world's thought that is beautiful. The truth in the algebra or in the grammar is real and useful, but it is not beautiful. As music is not sound, but only beautiful sound, as architecture is not the art of building, but of building beautifully, so literature is that thought or truth which comes to us commended by ornament. The novel is a book of truth or thought, ornamented by the presence of an attractive woman. As man has viewed and measured his world, the most attractive object under

245

the wide heavens is woman. Man thinks well of daisies and roses; he approves of the rainbow; he cannot but speak kindly of the ocean; but his words grow the most eloquent when he comes to speak about some woman of great absolute or alleged beauty.

Bowing before this shrine, Homer asked a Helen, a Briseis, a Penelope, to decorate his long stories; Sophocles had impressed into sweet duty the ‧matchless Antigone; Virgil had used Dido and Lavinia to act as colours for all his fields and clouds. When in the last lines of Virgil, the dying Turnus says to his rival: "Tua est Lavinia conjux," etc., "Lavinia is thy wife. Follow me no longer with thy vengeance," those words were prophetic of a day when a beautiful or frail woman would ornament a million books which should terminate each one in a wedding or a funeral. But Dante was yet living under the Greek and Latin administration. As Homer had asked Penelope to wave perpetually her flag of beauty, as Virgil had made Dido and Lavinia allure the world along over his lines, so Dante knew perfectly well that we should all pass more willingly through Hell and Purgatory, and through Heaven's gates, were we all aware that be-

fore us ran or floated a half divine Beatrice.
When in mature life, this Italian leader and
statesman determined to write an epic of
Italy, he could not forget that a beautiful
womanhood had often been the musical
accompaniment of human reflections. Manhood has also stood for an ornament, but man
as such has never equalled woman in the
ability to create or furnish a fine art. Dante
marked how the Homeric verses had made
thoughts plead and fail or triumph around an
attractive Helen. Had not Penelope inspired
a poem of general travel and adventure?
Had not Dido and Æneas helped Virgil to
make a continuity of beads of every size and
colour? Beatrice was so matchless in beauty
and character, and had been so exalted by
the absence the grave had brought, and she
was so precious to Dante's personal memory,
that his lips must have said: "I will ask her
to cast a charm over my survey of the Italian
state. She will exalt the reader while she
exalts me. She shall be a standard of virtues in comparison with which the blackness
of the age will remain undoubted. She will
gladly come back to me, for my misfortunes
will make all the scenes of my youth return,
and the past will fill a heart that no longer

possesses a future." Thus comes the book to us, a song indeed, but also a history, a philosophy, a sketch-book, an oration, a gallery of pictures, a synopsis of the Thirteenth Century.

Dante might well be called the first statesman of the Christian period. He came in advance of English and German letters, and although the Magna Charta had been created in England a few years before Dante was born, one of the twenty Oxford colleges had just been founded. It was a mere grammar school in those days. London and Paris were on the margin of that political light which was still shining out from the classic sun. Italy was nearer the centre. The politics of the Greeks and Romans flowed westwardly along with their languages, but they had not gone much beyond Florence when this great mind studied them.

In this continent when a great railway is opening out westwardly, industry, wealth, houses, streets, schools and churches spread out fan-like around the terminus of the highway. When after some years pass the road is carried a hundred miles onward, the local congestion diminishes and the power passing along the iron rail runs to another terminus

and repeats there its fan-like opening. Thus
in the Twelfth and Thirteenth Centuries the
vast Greek and Roman highway ended in
Florentine Principality, and as leaves and
blossoms grow where the vine is cut off, thus
a high politics threw out its leaves where the
Latin road ended or the Latin vine was
broken. Two parties arose, sometimes called
the Guelphs and Ghibellines, sometimes the
Whites and the Blacks. Called by whatever name, those two divisions were the same
old ones of all times. The Guelphs implied
the rule by constitutional law. Following
the example of nearly all great minds, Dante
espoused the broadest right and principle
and became the sturdy Republican of his
period. He argued for the separation of
Church from the State and won the fame of
orator before he won the fame of poet. He
antedated Count Cavour five hundred years,
and wrote down political maxims which are
now the practice of the whole Western world.

The treatise "De Monarchia" carried the
idea of constitutional politics so far that it
argued for a unity of all the states of Europe
with such home-rule here and there as a
change of circumstance should demand. The
monarchy Dante dreamed of differed little

from the England and America of to-day. To meet this unity of States the same broad thinker advocated a unity of language, and showed how the fourteen dialects of Europe were at bottom only one tongue. Of this unity of law and language and race the Papal absolutism was the one natural enemy. Hence came the parties, Guelphs (Papal) and Ghibellines (monarchical), hence the skirmishes and battles of centuries, hence the slaughter of the Albigenses which came a few years before the birth of the poet, hence the slaughter and exiles of the Huguenots long after, hence all the horrors which came between.

It was Dante's attachment to the idea of human unity that made him select Virgil and Statius as *dramatis personæ* in the poem in which the Christian Beatrice was to be the leading character. Such a grouping came from the feeling that genius and morality make all times and persons to be one. In Dante's visions Pagan and Christian move along side by side. David was crowned King of Israel while Æneas was landing in Italy, and Christ came into the world at a time when He could be aided by the reign of Cæsar Augustus. Plato, Socrates, Py-

thagoras and Cicero were the same in sub-
stance with the Fathers of the Church. In
the eternal world he saw Plato, the idealist,
and Aristotle, the realist, sitting down together in equal honour or imperfection.
Boethius, the philosopher, coming five hundred years after Christ, joined with the
pages of Cicero in making Dante declare
that philosophy had become the mistress of
his soul. As Solomon had long before
painted Wisdom as an attractive woman who
took her place near the city gates and uttered lessons to the passing throng, so Dante,
deeply coloured in all the profound thought
which lay between Plato and Boethius, declared his Beatrice to be the living emblem
of that wisdom of the world :

" O lady, thou in whom my hopes have rest,
   Who for my safety has not scorned, in hell
   To leave the traces of thy footsteps marked,
   For all mine eyes have seen, I to thy power
   And goodness virtue owe and grace. Of slave
   Thou hast to freedom brought me, and no means
   For my deliverance hast left untried.
   Thy liberal bounty still towards me keep
   That when my spirit which thou madest whole
   Is loosened from this body, it may find
   Favour with thee. So I my plea preferred ;
   And she so distant far, looked down,
   Smiled once and towards the eternal fountain turned."

The scene preliminary to this prayer seems
to take the poet away from the mere character of a lover and transform him into a
mind busy among the problems of Florence
and of society. Beatrice had vanished from
his side, and when he had cried out,
" Whither has she vanished ? " an aged man
appeared instead and replied that the loved
one had sent him to point out the higher
throne to which she had risen. So Dante
let eye run upward, throne above throne, and
there he beheld his idol high up among the
eternal truths and the infinite liberty. It is
not probable that Beatrice stood for any one
form of truth, that of religion or politics, but
for that philosophy which is the highest
form of truth and thought attainable in all
the departments of mental industry. She
was to Dante a living embodiment of what
our more abstract century has embodied in
the hymn " Nearer to Thee." Beatrice stood
for all height—political, ethical and religious.

With such internal reasons of being, this
poem began at once a career of influence.
It would not have created the Italian language had it not possessed an internal greatness which clothed its melodious words with
power. Dante did not make a language by

joining the dictionary to mere poetic beauty ;
he was made more powerful by his having
the courage and the statesmanship that could
attach language and beauty to what was
greatest in civilization. That which compelled one pope to forbid the reading of the
verses was the element in them which carried them along. It was known that Dante
had declined in anger a permission to return
to Florence if he would return a penitent
and pay also a fine. He said he was not so
earthen-hearted as to go back like a truant
schoolboy or as a criminal. He must return
in honour or not at all. He could see the
sun and stars when outside the city, and
could ponder over sweet truth under any
sky. Thus the poem rested upon funda-
mental truths and the person of a hero.

To the dignity of its themes the work
adds all the confessed elements of true poetry.
The art is a high art. The natural style of
Dante is as full of surprises as that of Hugo.
It is intense and condensed. Often a word
or a phrase rings out like a trumpet or the
discharge of a heavy gun, and then follows
the tranquillity of a few lines. One of his
cantos begins thus :

" Broke the dead stillness of my brain a

crash of heavy thunder." He arose and looked around. The reader is aroused along with the writer. The thunder was the only bell fit to awaken such a traveller in the Inferno. No rap on the bedroom door, no breakfast bell, would be adequate call for one who is to advance a few paces and find men and women in the regions of eternal grief. A crash of heavy thunder was just the awakening the traveller needed in that awful gulf. When the fact or event needs the softened speech of sympathy, the rude sounds all cease, and the poem runs along like the bird song in the "Siegfried" of Wagner.

To the now living reader of Dante the book has become only a treasure of detached gems. So many persons in the work are so unknown to us that but for humanity's sake we should not care whether the poet had sent them to heaven or hell. We cannot pass judgment upon their doctrines or their condition. It is necessary to leave many such matters with the artist; but at intervals all through the long creation come episodes that belong to the Nineteenth Century and Thirteenth alike. The continuity of the tale is gone, but there is a lapful of pearls now off

their silken string. When Dante speaks of
a forest in spring time it is for our hearts he
speaks. The woods is the one through which
we have all walked in some happy day of
perhaps early life.

> " Through that celestial forest whose thick shade
>   With living greenness the new coming day
>   Attempered, eager now to roam and search
>   Its limits round, forthwith I left the stream,
>   Through the wide woods leisurely my way
>   Pursuing o'er the ground which on all sides
>   Delicious odour breathed. A pleasant air
>   That intermitted never, never veered,
>   Smote on my temples—a mild wind
>   Of touch the softest, at which the boughs
>   Obedient all bent trembling towards that point
>   Where first the Holy Mountain casts its shade,
>   Yet were not so disordered but that still
>   Upon their top the feathered quiristers
>   Applied their wonted art, and with full joy
>   Welcomed those hours of prime, and warbled loud
>   Amid the leaves which to their happy notes
>   Keep tenour, just as from branch to branch
>   Along the piney forest, on the shore
>   Of Chassi rolls the gathering melody."

Dante knows just when silence is more
eloquent than speech. He detects those
moments when two or three words contain
more power than a hundred, but he also

knows of those places where speech is richer than silence, and the man who upon one page is as condensed as Tacitus becomes upon the next page as full and free as Virgil. He is as mutable as water, which is capable of acting either as dewdrop or as ocean.

His lessons as artist or painter, taken in his youth, may have added to his love of those pictures in which his verse abounds. As a painter he opens many a canto which he is to close as a philosopher :

" It hath been heretofore my chance to see
　　Horsemen with martial order shifting camp
　　To onset sallying or in muster ranged
　　Or in retreat sometimes outstretched for flight,
　　Light-armed squadrons and fleet foragers
　　Scouring thy plains, Arezzo, have I seen,
　　And clashing tournaments and telling jousts—
　　Now with the sound of trumpets, now of bells,
　　Drums or signals made from castled heights
　　And with inventions multiform, our own
　　Or introduced from foreign land."

The power of Dante to group details is not less than that of those illustrious successors which time brought, in Shakespeare and Milton. When Beatrice stood watching, to note on the horizon the chariot of Christ, she became a type of such gentleness and affection that the poet could but liken her to a little mother bird :

"Who midst a leafy bower
Has, in her nest, sat darkling through the night
With her dear brood, impatient to discern
Their looks again and to bring home their food,
In the fond search unconscious of all toil—
In the long meanwhile, on the boughs
That overhang the nest, with wakeful gaze
Watches for sunlight, nor till dawn
Removeth from the east her eager ken."

Here the "leafy bower," "the waiting in darkness," "impatient for light to reveal the hidden faces," the eagerness to bring home food, "the unconsciousness of toil," the "sitting towards the east" that she may detect the light sooner, watching for day on the leaves that overhang her nest, make up that richness which belongs to the universe of an Infinite Creator. The common mind can allude to a bird upon the nest and can join some humane associations for inculcating lessons of mercy to the wild boys of the street, but a Dante alone can grasp the entire scene and can make the soul of the little bird stand for that great human race which in the long night of earth watches for dawn, and in the long shadows turns the face forever towards the sunrise of a morrow. Dante's style is all through that of a brocaded silk. Five hundred years have separated us from much in the poem that was once powerful and beautiful, but enough remains to secure for the work a place among the most wonderful pieces in the literature of the entire world.

What ought to add value to the poem is the thought that it helped lead Europe out of error and to create for it those waves of light which soon began to roll after each other over Germany, France and England. The verses were perhaps most powerful in the Fourteenth Century. They were recited in the clubs and parlours of Italy and France, and were sung in the streets. They were so full of sentiment, thought and rapture that while they were laying the foundations of political law they were inspiring all the arts, and while they were the preludes of the Reformation in religion and politics they made Angelo and Raphael appear in the arena of beauty. These harmonious verses differed from these of Anakreon which would not sound anything but love. These Italian lines not only sang love as Greek or Latin sang it, but they made liberty as eloquent as love, and leave us to wonder whether Beatrice was not herself an emblem of that Supreme Wisdom, all whose ways are pleasantness and peace.

XII

MARTIN LUTHER[1]

HERE we are in the closing years of the Nineteenth Century. Beyond doubt it is the greatest Century ever lived by mankind. Some old periods were great in architecture, others in war, others in abstract philosophy, others in an ascetic religion like that of India, others in external magnificence like those of Babylon and Carthage, but this century contains all the valuable forms of eminence which marked the past, and to those forms of thought and sentiment it adds its own unrivalled stores. Compared with the present, old commerce and old philosophy and old industry and old science and old religion were only infants reaching out childish hands to play. We find ourselves on the banks of such a stream of intellectual and moral power as never flowed through the nations founded by the Pharaohs or conquered by Cæsar or coveted by the early popes.

[1] Born November 10, 1483 ; died February 18, 1546.

We dare not boast, for little of this triumph comes from us. As individuals we are only witnesses at the spectacle, without being ourselves the amazing scene. We are to add our souls to the vast fact, but it did not come from us. We are like the humble crowd which received and welcomed Jesus. He was greater than they. He arose in the far-off mountains and porches of meditation and study, and then moved down upon the common fields of Palestine. The crowd welcomed Him and afterwards became changed into His likeness. Thus our modern glory of politics and science and art and law and benevolence has flowed down to us, and we welcome it with many a hosanna, but instead of being its whole cause we are blessed forever if we are changed into its image. As the thick soil is formed by the leaves and grasses which fall upon the earth and dissolve into it, so the richness of our century is the result of that human foliage which budded and bloomed and perished long ago. How long the human race has thus been living and dying we know not, but it is possible that we are twenty thousand years away from the first prayers to God and from the first tears that ever fell upon a grave. If

Newton, while thinking of the stars, felt that he was only a child on the shores of a sea, so may we, in looking back at the spectacle of man, feel that we are only children standing by a measureless wave. Our hearts are emptied of all egotism, and from boasting we fall to praying for the privilege of helping onward the advancing world.

The causes of this stream are back of us. To enumerate them would be the study of the entire history of man. They must be passed by to make room for a single influence—that of some peculiar individual man. Some single, rare mind of man or woman appears upon the scene in this age or that and causes a commotion of ideas by its own momentum. It has not always been a man. The names of Esther and Zenobia and Roland and De Staël are enough to assure us that had not man fettered and degraded woman, power would have been seen in the whole past issuing from the lofty souls of woman and man. From the nature of society power has been developed in man, and his has been the hand that has made and unmade the most evil and the most good. If woman has been denied power she has thus escaped the charge of having brought so many nations to ruin. Man has touched all, and has ruined much upon which his hand has fallen. Babylon fell under his vices, Rome under his sin and war. But at times there has appeared a soul as full of momentum as an ocean wave. "Sons of God" these are called in the rich poetry of the Orient. We, too, would thus speak of all gifted ones had not our Northern zone carried us away from that highly wrought, emotional nature which traces quickly the glory of the Deity and of human life. The same parallels of latitude which separate us from the aromas of the warm lands, from the frankincense and myrrh, separate us also from their affectionate language, and we bury as a man one whom Arabia and Asia would have lamented as a "Son of God." To the power of climate and race to hush the words of poetry, perhaps also machines and inventions and discoveries are adding their temptation to us to look to these for help rather than to the individual soul. We may be transferring our love over to steam and electricity, and are yearly thinking less of such a living soul as that which we call Jesus, of Paul, or Savonarola, or Luther. If so, it is our error and our loss, for the truth

is that our world does not tremble under the
pulsations of the engine so much as under
the beatings of the heart, the rumbling of
the locomotive being heard not half so far
as the footstep of a great man.

Luther repeated history by being born in
humble life. The wheels of youth rest or
rust in riches; in poverty they all run.
Wealth says, How shall I enjoy myself?
Poverty says, What labour shall I perform?
Out of the former come those who play;
out of the latter those who work. But this
scarcity of money must be joined to a great
degree of sensibility and culture inherited
from ancestors or found in the earliest surroundings of youth. For if poverty alone
were able to make greatness the African
tribes and the Zulus should be supplying the
world with statesmen, and the mud huts of
New Mexico should be sending forth poetry.
That hardness of childhood that grows
mental force must be attached to an awakened mind; it must be a hardness like that
of Shakespeare and Franklin and Lincoln in
hearts surrounded by civilization. There are
women in India who have more sorrow than
fell to the lot of the Brontë sisters; but in
India the suffering is not joined to a cultured

brain. Thus it is hardship and civilization combined that make the wheels of the brain go. The infant Luther enjoyed such a two-fold impulse. Christ was indeed born in a manger, but that manger was carpeted with all the wisdom of the East, and canopied by the love of an enlightened mother, so that while the little body of Jesus was near the straw and hay His soul was where Greek and Roman and Hebrew wisdom and taste combined to make a new air. Thus Franklin and Lincoln were born in poverty of money but in the perfect splendour of liberty and education and hope.

Luther was the son of a slate-digger and cutter who had refinement enough to desire to educate his little boy up to the highest standard of the period. When the child was only six months of age the parents moved to where there could be found in a few years the good of education. Thus the natural power of the child enjoyed that advantage found in the ambition of its father. If it was not heir to gold, it was born to an estate of parental solicitude and ambition. Much of German eminence among men had come from the devotion of father and mother to the care of each child. As each Hebrew mother had a remote suspicion that perhaps her boy was to be the saviour of Israel, so each German parent easily reached the conclusion that the nation had long been waiting for his son to appear; and so far as lay in their power the German fathers and mothers urged their offspring onward towards a dreamed-of destiny. Stilling and Mozart and Beethoven and Goethe were not only born to great powers, but also were whipped to success by their fathers. All complain of the pitiless cruelty of their early surroundings. Stilling's father whipped him almost daily. To common cruelty the father of Beethoven added drunkenness; but yet so anxious was he that his son should become an extraordinary musician that he falsified regarding the child's age that he might seem the more a prodigy. In keeping with this record Luther came to the task of life miserably flogged all through his first ten years. And what omission of the birchen switch may have occurred at home was fully atoned for by the zeal of the village schoolmaster, and between the home and the schoolhouse no lesson of duty or piety remained free from this barbarous mode of enforcement.

In mature life Luther looked back with

something of sorrow upon such treatment— sorrow for himself and sorrow for the mistakes of those whom he deeply loved. He wrote: " My parents treated me so cruelly that I became timid. They felt that they were sincerely right, but they had no discernment of character that would have enabled them to know when and upon whom and how punishment should be inflicted." While our times have no sympathy with this brutality it cannot but look with approval and delight upon the parental care and ambition which encompassed all these great children in their old German homes. In framing an explanation of many of the leading men of the whole past we must find a part of the causes of things to rest in the culture and ambition of the father and mother. Cicero's father moved to Rome that he might educate his boy. Augustine's mother cared for her child with an infinite enthusiasm until he had reached almost middle life. She lived for him alone.

Thus out of a poor home as to money, but out of a good home as to judgment and ambition and piety, came upward the mind which was to turn the stream of the Western thought and life. In imagination we can picture this youth of fourteen leaving his home that he might attend a school that should prepare him for the university. He performed the journey on foot and carried in a knapsack all his worldly possessions. Rude as his home had been, the scene before him was so dreary that it made the cottage behind him seem an enchanted ground; and as he moved away from the charm of the one and towards the hardship of the other the tears rolled down his cheeks. Once located at the school he sang songs under the windows of the rich and supported himself by what small coins fell at his feet. He performed this musical circuit thrice each week. At last his voice, rich in itself, but made more touching by his poverty, won the sympathy of a woman of wealth, and out of these songs under a window came a woman's kindness, which paid for four years of education in that school and for a home in the house won by his music. You can recall the picture. A boy singing in front of the quaint house of Dame Ursula Cotta. A kind face comes to the window and looks and listens. Weeks and months pass and by degrees the dame begins to wish that the little Martin Luther would come again.

Each week the coins the kind hand tosses out increase in size or in number. At last the woman talks with the boy, and hears the simple story of his struggles and hopes. She at last says: "Well, you need not sing for money any more. I shall help thee onward."

It must be a matter of conjecture what were the songs he thus offered along the streets. The Minnesingers who went from place to place with their love-songs died away in the Fourteenth Century. The Sixteenth Century was in the outset religious in Germany. Michelet says Luther inherited poverty and piety. But after all is said regarding the religious drift and even superstition of the times, there remained much margin in mind and heart to be filled up with the common songs of sentiment and passion. As mankind never becomes too pious to fall in love, it is not probable that any age ever passed which sang only hymns in the streets. Luther may have offered some religious piece at some appropriate lattice, but when the face half visible showed features of beauty and youth the sentimental music of the universal heart must have brought him the most money. This Martin played well on the guitar, but his voice needed no accompaniment.

Mark the quality of his studies in these formative years,—grammar, rhetoric, poetry and music. Upon such a course our age has not made much improvement. Our period offers more facts—those of science and history—but it offers less of inspiration. Facts are a poor substitute with the young mind for rhetoric and poetry because these are the wings of the soul, whereas facts can be acquired and retained by a man without a soul. Either method is in itself defective. A perfect course would be that which should combine the acquisition of knowledge with the highest development of language and rhetoric and the imagination. It was the good fortune of this German youth, and of the world through him, that he became strong in music and poetry and language, for these helped him to rise to an enthusiasm which was able to burn like an eternal fire. When the times needed impetuosity Luther became impetuous ; when inspiration was asked for this man became inspired. Vast learning would have quieted that heart which was needed not as a library, but as a burning torch.

Towards such a restless zeal these studies all pointed. Poetry underlies more heroism than learning alone can boast. It, only, rises above the common things of the shop and market-place, and perceives the immensity of human and divine affairs. The heart, which could proceed to the city of Worms to meet perhaps death, was the heart which could, the day before the journey began, compose the words and the music of a hymn that seemed fully able to sustain its author. The poet was the hero.

> " A tower safe our God is still ;
> A trusty shield and weapon ;
> He'll help us clear from all the ill
> That hath us overtaken."

Thirty-six such lines as these sung in the outset and chanted in the choir of the soul were the band of music for that march of one man against the potentates of the age. His prose was all ornamented, like a wall covered with vines. Speaking of a tree laden with ripe fruit, he said : " Had Adam not sinned, we should have seen the beauty of these things ; every bush and shrub would have seemed more lovely than though it were made of gold and silver. It is really more lovely, but we are stupid as beasts. God's power and wisdom are shown in the smallest flowers. Painters cannot rival their colour, nor perfumers their sweetness; green, yellow, crimson, blue and purple—all growing out of one earth. We trample upon the lilies as though we were so many cows."

Poetry is not in itself a divine power, for Cowper and Wordsworth could not have led in a revolution. Neither could Virgil. But when the poetic sentiment is joined to a great soul it becomes an irrepressible impulse. It does not sit down and write verses, but it detects the joys and griefs, the rights and wrongs of the people, and weeps and hopes while mere learning reads or sleeps. Like Dante and Angelo and Milton, Luther had power as well as fancy. His success as a student was very great. He surprised his instructors. He was quick and strong in debate, original, full of vivacity, rich in the German language, and was perhaps the first great orator to venture forth upon philosophical debate in the tongue of the people. He was a Latin scholar by the time he was twenty, but he preferred the German; he brought forward a revolution in speech before he led in religion, and from him came the dialect of Schiller and Goethe and Jean Paul Richter!

It was the design of the young man to study law. It is singular that neither Luther's father nor Valcin's held theology or the priesthood in much esteem. Each father was heart-broken over the religious drift of his son. A comment this, not upon the piety of the fathers, for they were deeply devout, but upon the condition of the clergy in those days. The vices of the age had made their black mark upon many of the monastics. Many monks who were not dissolute were simply lazy beggars. Luther, with all his lofty powers, was to take the path of the law. It offered some honour and some industry and money, and much less hypocrisy. Towards this the father pointed, and towards it the son turned his face.

For the law the youth at last had no heart. Pure and innocent himself, Luther saw the Church through a clear, divine air. Its music charmed him. And, moreover, there often come to young hearts melancholy years. It would seem that early life should produce nothing but smiles and laughter. Youth is thus pictured by painter and poet, and in general it is full of joy or peace; but for some unknown cause Nature inserts a melancholy year between ten and twenty-five. Tears come easily. The heart is morbidly sensitive. It writes farewell notes to friends. The soul loves to creep into its corner and distrust the voice of love. A few hearts thus in life's sweet morning wholly break, and suicide ends the scene. The wave of sadness rose high around this gifted youth. The storm may have come from injured health, but more probably it came from unseen recesses in the spirit. No path of duty seemed clearly defined. But as he walked in a field with a fellow student a bolt of lightning killed the companion in an instant, and left Luther still in the world. Full of superstition the astounded youth fell on his knees and vowed all his powers to God. He entered a convent, and thus began the Reformation. It was kindled by a flash of lightning.

A fact must be mentioned here which will betray at once the need of an overthrow of the past. The cup of folly was full. The people had been long enough fed upon the marvellous stories of ascetics and idlers and miracle-mongers. Luther went into the convent taking with him two books, the only books, perhaps, he possessed. What were they? Were they the Testaments full of the simple godlike life of Jesus and of the labours and teachings and glories of St. Paul and St. John and the lofty strains of Job and David and Isaiah? Oh, no! This educated youth of the Sixteenth Century took into the convent with him Virgil and Plautus! The secret of the Reformation is out. Luther had been reared to manhood in the church without ever having seen the Bible. It was almost a lost volume. Where existing, it was in a foreign tongue. Custom of the monks had become the standard of morals and the basis of all doctrine.

Virgil and Plautus were pleasant books, but not adequate to the production of a civilization. Æneas and Dido figured largely in the oddities of St. Augustine while he was in pagan clouds. But, as it was, Luther took into the convent too much logic and rhetoric and fervour, for the most aged monks in the monastery soon became alarmed at the life and wisdom and force of the new comrade, and they held a secret meeting to determine how to check the unsaintly manners of the young devotee. A venerable ecclesiastic declared such a love of books to be sinful, that it elevated too much the individual mind when it ought to sit prostrate, meekly submissive to the high dispensation of the superiors! Luther was condemned to be the man-of-all-work for the convent, and for three years he swung the broom, carried the wood, scrubbed the stairs, and then with the company of a pack-mule, he begged food from door to door. "This," said the reverend theologians, "will break his spirit of self-importance."

In their prophecy they were mistaken, for the same mind which had combined drudgery and study in boyhood could do so again in mature life. The stream of Luther's piety and logic and study ran straight on, his hours with the pack-mule being hours of meditation, and more valuable than hours with the monks. In his mind the truths of religion gradually fell into a shape quite different from the forms and customs which had come down from the dark ages.

All gifts of learning and genius would have been vain had not Luther possessed piety. His soul was sincerely religious. God and Jesus Christ were loved, and lived for, and trusted. Christianity was not a form, but it was his joy and his hope. In fervour

he was more like Mme. Guyon and Fénelon
to come after him than like those who had
passed before him. His hymns were not
full of theology but of affection :

> Thou strong defense, Thou Holy Light,
> Teach us to know our God aright,
> And call Him Father from the heart ;
> The Word of Life and Truth impart
> That we may love not doctrines strange,
> Nor e'er to other teachers range,
> But Jesus for our Master own
> And put our trust in Him alone.
> Hallelujah, Hallelujah !
>
> Thou sacred Ardour, Comfort Sweet,
> Help us to wait with ready feet
> And willing heart at Thy command,
> Nor trial fright us from Thy band.
> Lord, make us ready with Thy power—
> Strengthen the flesh in weaker hour,
> That as good warriors we may force
> Through life and death to Thee our course.
> Hallelujah, Hallelujah !

Such was the personal approach of Luther
towards an unseen but vast work. His
learning, his natural power, his honesty, his
fervour, his stubborn will and his unequalled
courage fitted him to be a leader from darkness to light. He was one of those whose
life shines in history like a sun in the sky.

XIII

VICTOR HUGO [1]

IT is common to look upon France as the home of atheism. But such an estimate of the condition of faith in that country is far from being true. Of the 36,000,000 of the French population 34,000,000 are Roman Catholics; a little over 1,000,000 are Protestants, thus leaving 1,000,000 within which all the forms of anti-religious sentiment are to enact their various parts. In a census taken a few years ago only 85,000 persons were recorded as having no belief or an anti-Christian belief. Thus out of 36,000,000 only one person in 4,000 is to be quoted as indifferent or opposed to the forms and ideas of religion. From the common fame about France, with the history of the Revolution and Reign of Terror and Commune, we have all felt that this was the one godless nation of Europe. Against this common fame we are met by the fact that of the population of France

[1] Born February 26, 1802; died May 22, 1885.

more than ninety-nine per cent. are Christians.

But this surprising fact will not explain all and contradict all, because we must remember that the world is not governed by majorities, not even by so large a majority as ninety-nine per centum. France has, in one instance, been atheistic for a brief period, but it was such by a *coup d'état*. In that method of seizing an empire sometimes a thousand brave men will equal a million citizens. For the most part Paris has been France; just as the city of Mexico has always been the whole nation. At a recent Mexican election of high officials not one man in ten took the trouble to go to the polls to vote. The voting was all done by a few thousands who had some individual interests in the result. Thus in France, Paris has generally attended to all the political business; and thus a group of a million and a half has really stood for the entire mass of thirty-six millions.

Of the enormous religious population thirty-five millions are Roman Catholics, and the tendency of that church has always been to sink the individuality of the man, to make the common millions full of timidity and obsequiousness, and to concentrate in

ecclesiastical potentates what personal heroism the Church could produce. We have in
France the most decidedly Roman Catholic
country in the world; the one empire to
which the Pope has always looked for support, Spain not being excepted. But in
battling against rationalism and what little
atheism there existed, these ecclesiastical
millions could do but little. At any time of
the Revolution Paris contained only a little
more than half a million of inhabitants.
Thus the enormous throng of nominal Christians was spread out in a nation whose
domain was 600 miles long by 400 miles
wide. Furthermore, of this religious population about one-third of those over six years
of age could not read or write. As there
were no railways or telegraphs it is almost
certain that the changes of political situations
lay in the hands of the great central city and
a half score of large towns.

Thus it came to pass that the few atheists
who finally figured in the Revolution were
concentrated in Paris, and were men of great
daring because they were the children of the
new thought and new mental power which
at the same time had made our Paine and
Franklin and the great deists of Europe.

The French Revolution did not come from irreligion, but from the most awful and long-continued oppression and criminality of the throne. The Roman Catholics hated the Government with a hatred based upon robbery and starvation. A terrible famine had made many thousands of beggars take refuge in Paris, and when the States General was called to attempt to secure some rights for the people these were in the city ready for anything that might offer hope of a change, for a change could not be for the worse. In the States General elected, the first class contained 291 clergymen, in the third class there were nearly 500 of the better members of the people. It was in the chaos which came along slowly that a few atheists got possession of the reins of power. Even this group was divided, for Robespierre declared himself against Danton and avowed himself as eager to set up a government which should confess God and the immortality of the soul. Foreign nations were making use of the sorrows of France to invade her territory, and in the midst of such a babel some brilliant atheists passed into power. But this reign was of short duration. This godless party became the disgust of the millions of Roman-

ists and Protestants. The atheists were to
erase the history of the world, and they ordered a new chronology to begin. They
were to date letters and documents with the
year "1." Having ample power thus to
name their first year they had no method of
establishing a succession, and year "1" never
advanced to year "2."

These statements seem necessary to remind us that Victor Hugo was not the product of an atheistic nation, because there was
or is no such a nation; but rather was he the
true child of that great rationalism which
began to purify the air in the Christian
Pascal and the deist Voltaire. The Roman
Church would not open to admit a new truth
or to reject an old error. The great mass of
religious barnacles the holy ship had cultivated and carried along in the Dark Ages it
attempted to carry along through the Seventeenth and Eeighteenth Centuries. It denied
they were barnacles, and called them pearls.
There was no progress of knowledge possible
in that denomination. This fact made necessary a belief that should be not only outside
of the Church, but even full of wit and re-
sistless logic against that venerable organism.

The Protestant forms of Christianity had

been less hostile to reason, but they had a horror of the hearts of the children of the Pope. An outside religion thus became necessary unless men would consent to dispense with the use of reason. This was so large a price to pay that minds by nature religious were compelled to live and die with a faith partly beautiful but partly injured by neglect and lifelong argument. Some few, like Lamartine, stood with one foot on the old altar, but these were detained there more by the French romance than by any regard for the moss-covered human theology. The sentiments detained many to whom the reason was pointing a different road.

What a brilliant group was this! Mme. De Staël and Napoleon were in it. There stood also Victor Cousin, who perhaps more than any man of our century helped turn the young generations of France away from the philosophy of atheism and towards that of God. He was imprisoned for a short time by the influence of the priesthood, but he came forth to stand wholly outside the earthly churches, yet evidently wholly inside of the church of the heavenly Father. Under his touch religion became founded upon the deepest reason, and was seen as the ab-

solute fountain of human greatness. He
was a pupil of the Royer-Collard, who spent
his life in a high philosophy drawn from all
the noble minds, from Reid of Scotland back
to Plato of the Greeks. Time would fail us
to mark those great names which were compelled, passing life in France, to cherish their
religious sentiments out in that open air
where the spirit of reason could associate
with the spirit of worship, and where man
could be true to his God without being false
to himself.

In the midst of this large class, but more
grand than numerous, stood Victor Hugo in
his long life, and now in his grave he sleeps
with them. He was the ripe fruit of that
Voltairism which could not call folly by the
name of inspiration, nor a career of sins and
errors by the name of infallibility; but to the
strength of Voltaire he added the rich poetry
of Lamartine, and thus he contained the virtues of two great intellects. He bids us remember that France produces two kinds of
human beings: the luxuriant animal and the
luxuriant soul—men who will deny the being
of a God and live for only the object of
transient sense; and men who will place before us a religion full of fervour and colour-

ing, a religion as rich as the many-tinted
window of a cathedral, when seen while the
highest music is sounding a vesper for the
heart. French religion, when it has come
to us through some of its noblest minds,
has come in a most impressive form, having
in it much of that delicacy and ornament
which distinguishes the French mind from
the mind that speaks and argues under more
northern skies. Chateaubriand, although a
Romanist, was so modernized by the re-
flex influence of the Rationalists, that his
"Genius of Christianity" came to the
world more like a lofty poem than like a
treatise from a theologian. His wide reading, his travels in all lands, his dreamings in
the forests of America, when General Washington became his friend, his poetic medita-
tions in the land of Christ and the apostles,
his poems—"Atala" and "René"—his novels, betrayed and created an eloquence which
made Christianity repose upon the day of un-
belief like the rainbow upon black clouds.
The general truths of religion came from his
hand as beautiful and pure as the marbles
from the sculptor's studio. The civilized
world had never before seen the height and
depth of the sentiment of God, the Son of

God, and immortal life. He had been a rationalist, and almost a free-thinker, but he returned to the established Romanism as being the best hope of humanity.

In looking at these forerunners of Hugo, we must not omit the name of Lamennais. He, too, was one of the eloquent souls for which French religion has been very remarkable. Lamennais remained in the mother church until he had reached his forty-sixth year. But in the later of those years, he had with so much power advocated liberty of religion, freedom of speech, that when he announced his withdrawal from Rome he had not far to go. The volume he published at the time went through a hundred editions before its grand style and language sank into silence. It was the song of the new world.

These names will serve to remind us that France is not atheistic; but she has come to that condition of education and liberty which makes her greatest minds prefer to stand outside of the Church and perhaps aloof from the public religion. The Roman Church in its refusal to learn the truth has become a sanctuary whose doors open outward, that those in may escape. It reverses in France the gospel imagery of a feast to which the multitude were urged to come in; here this feast is seen and known to be over, and the honourable guests are compelled to retire. Many who remain within, priest and people, are in full sympathy with the rationalism and republicanism on the outside. When Lamennais advocated liberty and equality the lower clergy were on his side; the higher ecclesiastics were the ones to oppose his liberal views. Even now when riots and barricades are prevalent in Paris, the men of no religion are found side by side with those who are nominal followers of Christ, all these meeting on the common ground of hunger, nakedness, and injustice.

Victor Hugo comes up before us with the same ardent belief in God which has marked many of the greatest men of France. He is seen standing for a great transition period in which old Romanism and old Calvinism are dying, and something better is being elaborated in the mind and heart of the new epoch. Although his mind was set to romance and poetry like that of Lamartine, he possessed more of unbridled power, and what he uttered regarding God added to the sweetness of the poetic the roll of thunder. His short and sharp sentences fell not like an argument but like the sentence of a final judgment. When the Deity was introduced in novel or drama or speech no apologies were made for His entrance. He came in like a king. No modern writer made so little use of mitigating terms. The terms "peradventure," "perhaps," "presume," "suppose" were seldom asked to perform any service. Waterloo was lost "because of God"; Napoleon "vexed God"; "the shadow of an enormous right hand rested upon Waterloo"; "God passed over it." In the last words of Jean Valjean this Supreme Ruler enters the scene beautifully, but with no modifying particles of doubt or contingency. "Such are the distributions of God. He is on high. He sees us all, and knows what He is doing among the great stars."

That individuality which made this great man seem an egotist clothed him with power when amid the world-wide themes of action and opinion. He seldom came to a contemplation of himself, and hence his egotism consumes but few sentences in his mass of written thought. He should be forgiven, because the mental quality which was sometimes egotistic was in most hours the movement of a powerful will and an open heart incapable of concealment. He made himself visible only at rare intervals, compared with his grand public presentation of humanity and the fact and presence of God. In one of his novels the world's miserable stand forth in such visible and lovable and beseeching attitude that the living and advancing race will not soon lose sight again of the unhappy. He was a painter greater than those who have covered canvas with their conceptions, for while Parrhasius could not paint a groan, the art of Victor Hugo was fully equal to that task. His language caught up the troubles of the multitude and made this groan sound in the two hemispheres—a pathetic and solemn tone struck from a loud-sounding harp. He also could paint the gladness of the soul, but no musician, no sculptor, no architect, no painter, could say of human happiness what Hugo said: "Our joys are shaded. The perfect smile belongs to God alone."

In this transition period, while pulpit and church were seeking better definitions of their old terms, and asking Whence came man—from a Creator, or from inanimate causes, and by what path? Hugo was busy with the actual world applying the ideas of

Jesus on behalf of the orphans and widows—
"those formidable pleaders"—made by the
armed Napoleons, on behalf of black slave
and white, the oppressed of the whole world.
What a poet was he compared with the Greek
Anacreon! For this sensual Pagan said,
his forehead crowned with leaves and his
harp in his hand, "Farewell all truth, philosophy, and heroes; I shall sing only of
love." But the modern poet said: "I will
forget love, family, childhood, song, and
leisure that I may sing for the welfare of
the oppressed." Beyond doubt his fifty
years of sympathetic opinion and eloquent
speech have entered into the better laws and
kinder philanthropy of the century.

We are thankful for the more symmetrical
men of the times, for the calmer poets, the
more careful philosophers, the men of profound learning and of childlike modesty,
thankful for those minds which lead us inside the sanctuary and whose prayers and
hymns keep up the never dying flame upon
the altar, thankful for the great good done
by the Calvinists and the Romanists, and to
all those flowing tides of gratitude we may
add a feeling of gladness that such a man as
this Victor came such as he was and passed

along through our century by the pathway
now marked by his footsteps. His intense
manner aroused a sleeping myriad. His
funeral in France attended in some manner
by a million persons tells us how his writings
and presence have affected that vast multitude that knows the sorrow of poverty, the
cruelty of despotism, and the sweet of liberty and equality. In that great moment
the Pantheon was secularized that so great a
friend of mankind might rest in a great
tomb. Instead of being secularized it was
rather made more religious by receiving
within its walls that forehead that was fur-
rowed by frowns against wrong, those lips
that had long been eloquent over the being
of God.

In his prophecy and sublime prose-poem
upon God, Ezekiel many times addresses the
son of man to urge him to mark and adore
that Divine Providence from whom came
the mystery of life. "Son of man" is a
phrase that stands for the average power and
nobleness of human nature. It points out
man in his youth, in his romance, reverence,
love, ambition, vivacity, logic, and hope.
Infancy with its weakness has passed away,
age with its decline has not come. Christ

took this title as a part of His honour, but He was also the son of God. Looking into our period we can detect here and there the "sons of men." Victor Hugo was one of these. He was the son of our century—a full expression of the science, reason, art, benevolence, and broad religion that have taken deep root in its rich soil; he was the full expression of the millions who are weeping their way along as they journey from poverty's cradle to poverty's grave; he was the son of the rationalism of Europe which has filled the era with great minds able to live great lives; he was the son of America in his devotion to a universal liberty and equality, a man reared upon the truths which made all those statesmen who are dear to hearts this side the sea; he was a son of France in his passionate imagery, fancy, and in his matchless language; a son of religion, too, for going out of the doors of the old Church he did it to enter at once the holier Temple of the Almighty. As some one has said, "He turned his back to the Church that he might turn his face to God."

With history full of such names, with the air full of gratitude for such lives and full of lamentation for such graves, with these pictures before them of colossal minds extracting happiness and power from a divine faith, the young men of our day should feel that atheism possesses no intellectual charm; that religion in its essence is a height to which even genius may be glad to climb.

The Atheists recently attempted to hold a general meeting. It was to be in Rome, that it might seem more like a triumph of a proud reason over a superstitious faith. But it failed. Not a single delegate from all England was present—few from any point. There is not that in atheism that can inspire the heart. Men have made long pilgrimages, have journeyed in hunger and storm, but this travel has never been towards an empty life and the death of a brute, but always towards a God or the tomb of Him who said, "I am the resurrection and the life." God is the life of the heart.

May our century rear out of its measureless resources more great natures like that of Victor Hugo; men who will make humanity sound forth in grand music, and who, with an inspired mantle, will smite the stream of atheism until its waters shall part and open up for our millions of youth an easy pathway between their souls and God!

Index

Index

Index

Index

Index

Index

Index

Printed in the United States of America